Joseph N. Rose

Joseph Nelson Rose Letters to Walter Deane, 1888-1929

Joseph N. Rose

Joseph Nelson Rose Letters to Walter Deane, 1888-1929

ISBN/EAN: 9783337393960

Printed in Europe, USA, Canada, Australia, Japan

Cover: Foto ©ninafisch / pixelio.de

More available books at **www.hansebooks.com**

I have destroyed most of my correspondence with J. N. Rose as it has been of a personal nature.

W. Deane,

May 22 / 1908.

Washington D.C.
Dec. 27th, 888

My dear Doane:

Your letter was received more than two months ago. I should have been more [prompt?] but my time has been pretty well taken up since coming here.

Yes I supposed the cards would be a surprise to you. It was a very quiet little wedding; a few relatives of [Mr N.C.?] & wife. By the way this was the same [room?] [I?] [buried?] [from?] [to?] his wife 15 years [before?].

[Dr Vesey?] has some good [g...?] & [...] I think it will pay [...] [...] a bundle

down. I think it would
be just as well to send direct
to the Dr. I will send you
these same answers when I can
but I tell you it pretty scarce.
Our Umbelliferae paper will soon
be out and of course you will
receive a copy.
I am enjoying my work here
very much. I am preparing
a little paper on Coreopsis which
will appear soon.
If I can do anything for
you please let me know.
Give my kind regards to Mrs Deam,

Resp'y
J. N. Rose

Dr Kennedy has just called on me
He leaves on Monday

Washington D.C.
Jan 7th /889

My dear Deane:

Your letter should have been answered sooner. I am sorry no grasses have yet been sent to you. I spoke to the Doc'or about getting them out but he said he would do it and I have spoken to him several times but he is so busy. As I have nothing to do with the grasses I wish you had written direct to the Dr. But I will try once more for you.

Did you get Ef Smith's book on "Peach Yellows"? Dr V. will have a book out on grasses in a few days. If you do not get one in side of two weeks let me know.

I suppose you have gotten Mr.
Brandegee's fine paper on "Plants
from Baja California." You see
my new Lombardspruce?

At the very last I had to
give up my trip to C.

Prof Coulter is to be with me for
a month and will be here in a few days.

Yes we have a fine boy, over
4 months old. I was "there" in Washington when the young man came
and did not get away until he was
a month old. My wife is quite
well now. She was getting along
very nicely after baby came until
she was taken with a second attack
of Rheumatic fever which lasted six
weeks. I spent my vacation at
her bedside caring for her. But

As I said she is quite
well again and looking after
what she considers the finest baby in
Washington. She intends writing
to Mrs Deane very soon.
    We both send kindest regards
to you & yours
                Respt ly
                  A. K. Rose

Washington D.C.
May 29th 1881

My dear Dean:

Our present plans put us in Cambridge some time Wednesday, June 5th. I anticipate a very pleasant but busy visit. I will bring from Coville a good specimen of Phacelia?? in flower & fruit for you and Dr. Watson.

I hope you are well again by this time.

Hastily
J.N. Rose

Washington D.C.
June 23rd/89

My dear Deane:

Your card came just as we were leaving.

The arrival in W. Wednesday and I reported at headquarters at once. Dr. Vasey was much pleased with my work & has intimated that a similar trip is not far in the future.

Yes it was the "Agriculture Grasses of U.S." I had in mind.

I brought home some of Lepidium ruderale and found we only had specimens from the Philadelphia station.

By the way I have just received the official announcement that Wabash

Had you heard that the Western Botanists were forming a "trust." Brandegee & Mrs. Curran have united forces for life.

The public announcement has just been made that our friend Coville is engaged.

Miss Vasey was much pleased with your shadow.

If anything of interest comes in I will remember you.

Mrs. Rose wishes to be remembered to you & Mrs. Deane.

As always
J. N. Rose

Washington D.C.
July 17th 1889

My dear Deane;

On coming back yesterday I found your two letters & postal on my table and now hasten to answer. Mrs Rose and I have just been to Indiana for a little rest. I spent Sunday with Coulter. Monday we broke ground for the supplement to "North American Umbelliferae".

Of course *Carum Carui* should come in the manual. Have you a good specimen for the herbarium?

Dr. Vasey left last night for a six weeks trip through the west.

As regards your grasses as follows
1 *Poa caesia* var. *strictior*
2 *P. serotina*

Have I told you that I had been made 1st assistant with an increase of $200.00 since I returned. The department was greatly pleased with my effort. It will appear in the Smithsonian — write very soon now.

Coville's address is F. V. Coville, Washington D.C. Agriculture Depart. & he will be very glad to hear from you.

As ever
J. N. Rose

Washington D.—
July 29th '89

My dear Dean;

I have just been looking up the Agriculture Reports. and find that 1847 is the oldest. If I remember right—you have this report.

The indications are that I may have to come to Cambridge again this fall. I am getting some nice material together. My report has unavoidably been delayed but will soon be out.

What is Dr. Kennedy address and I will also send Judge Churchill a copy.

If I find any thing new about him I will let you.

As ever J. F. ____

Botanical Division
Sep 2nd /89

My dear Deane:

Your note came last night.

I should have answered your last note but Dr. Vasey is away and I know nothing about grasses; so he has not yet seen your grass.

I am very busy and have been hard at work all summer. I may be up to Cambridge in two or three weeks.

Palmer & Orcutt are sending me some good things from California. You do not care for anything so far west?

By the way a correspondent writes me of some good finds in Indiana and says "perhaps a new species". Specimens will come to me. This comes in your range doesn't it? I am quite anxious to see what they gotten out there. I thought I knew the Indiana Flora pretty well. I will let you know if it is anything of real interest.

My paper has been delayed but will be ready in a few days.

Dr. Vasey is in California and I am "Acting Botanist."

I will spend a part of the fall with Coulter. If there is anything you want I will send it to you, if we have it.

We are getting in a great amount of material this season.

I am glad to know yours are having such a good vacation. I wish I might have been there to botanize with you.

As ever

J. N. Rose

Washington D.C.
Nov 27/89

My dear Dean:

Your card just at hand. Dr. Vasey will send you the grasses soon.

You seemed not to understand me about J. Donnell Smith's. He have dedicated a new genus to him; the plants are now in the hands of Foxon & we will have a fine flora. I will soon have ready an other interesting flora both of which will be sent to you.

Either Dr. Vasey or I will be up to Cambridge in two or three weeks. I hope to see you.

Prof. Coulter has just spent a week with me. Look out for more on Halfsia in Bot. Gazette.

and also re Col. Read, &c.

Mr. Canby spent a day with me last week.

I mean to write very soon again. Mrs. Rose wishes to be remembered to you & Mrs Deane.

Very hastily
I. W. Rose

Washington D.C.
Dec. 3rd, 88[?]

My dear Deane,

I had not heard of your good father's death but I knew he had been very poorly for a long time and I was not surprised to hear that he had passed away. I remember meeting him once and thinking then what a pleasant old gentleman he was. I can hardly appreciate your loss, for I never knew what it

Mrs. Rose & I extend to you our sympathy at this time.

Your friend
J. N. Rose

Washington, D.C.
Dec 8th '89

My dear Keane:

I send you by this mail one other Umbellifer (paper) containing a number of new species. I have ready another pinch of new species.

I send you my notes of a hundred new species and [await] your careful consideration of [same].

Very truly
J. N. Rose

Perennial: stems about 2° ong., prostrate becoming erect, glabrous except at top (here a little pubescent); dichotomously branched; lower leaves then pedately parted, upper ones palmately; mouth oval, somewhat open, two lipped, entire (that is not toothed); "eye" blue, flowers 3'
Plate I (now in the hands of Rice)
Habitat: On the banks of Deer Creek Carroll Co, Ind.
Collectors: Dr Marrow & Nurse Kearns
   Aug 27/89
Remarks It is perhaps to be regretted that but a single specimen of this rare & beautiful Rose was collected and hence there can be no distribution. The specimen is kept in a Washington Nursery where some very interesting physiological experiments are being carried on.

Return this letter from
Rose, & then you'll see
if I think it is a very
good joke —

If new we propose the following name.
Rose(a) § Sims(ia) non Bens Joseph n sp.

Washington D.C.
June 11th

My dear Dean:

Thank you for Carex Com.
You know I never name an
Umbellifera without fault still
I think your plant is
Ptychotis Peters of by the of DC Prodromus
but according to B.&H. it goes
into Carum and the oldest
name seems to be C. Bunius L. of
S. Europe. How & why it get
up in N.B. I don't know.
Find out what you can about it.
I think we will have to make
a note of it. Coulter will be
here tomorrow & I will have
him look at it. I feel like
steal your plant.

Dr. Vasey's wife is very sick and he is not at the office now.
Have your *Shortia*. When you thank the Doctor for naming your grasses tell him you would like one; he will gladly send it. He has some beauties.

His Grass rod is out. Look for your travity.

The new Umbel is <u>Arracacia Brandegei CR.</u>

Hastily
J. N. Rose

Here are some fronds.

Washington D.C.
Feb 4th 1890

My dear Dean:
Your letter came this morning. Yes poor Knowlton has lost his good wife who leaves behind a little girl but 15 months old. I came up with him this morning: he tries to be bright & cheerful. He will remain in the city. A letter would reach him at the National Museum. You will have to thank some other friend for the Star.

Poor Coulter was called home Saturday night saying that his wife is very sick. We have not heard from him yet.

My good friend Canby will

be in Cambridge in a week or so. I hope you may see him.

I suppose your plants will come in time but things look forbidding. They were mislaid during a much needed cleaning and I have looked in vain for them. I am very sorry but still think they will be found.

Dr. Vasey is getting ready your grasses to day.

Hope & pray are both quite well

Your friend
J. W. Ross

Washington
Feb. 11th, 1890

My dear Deane:

I send you today the grasses & return your own. I hope you will find them satisfactory.

Very truly
F. L. Scribner
[Asst.] Botanist

Washington D.C.
Feb 12th 1898

My dear Dean:

I am afraid the Boston P.M. has got the best of you at least it looks that way.

I send you the latest ruling on the matter. I don't think it right. Some one ought to look into the matter.

Yes labels go with specimens. You will find it mentioned in the Gazette some where.

Hastily
J N Rose
Asst Botanist

Washington DC.
April 10th, 1890

My dear Dean;
  Your card tonight added another prick to my conscience for the careless manner I have treated your last letter.

  My wife is just recovering from a very serious illness. She was able to be down to dinner yesterday; the first time for almost two weeks.

  I am very busy, never had so much to do. I don't think I will have time to take any vacation this year. Palmer has sent in a big box of cactus from LaPaz Low Cal. A couple new genera have already appeared.

I will have some nice things in the March Gaz.

The Canby I wrote you about was W. M. Canby Wilmington Del. A great friend of Dr Gray.

Of course you saw Coulter the other day.

How do you like the new Manual?

We find a great pleasure in our boy. He grows fast, is very fair with blue eyes. He is the pet of this end of Washington.

About that Carume. Did Brettni collect any more of it. I would so much like a specimen. I will look it up in the morning & add what data I have.

as ever J. W. R—

Washington D.C.
May [?]/[?]

My dear Dean:

I All goes well I expect to bring [wife?] & [son?] to Cambridge next month with me. It seems best for the interests of the Agriculture department that I again visit the Gray Herbarium.

I was wrong about Coulter going to Cambridge. He left me here saying he was going direct to Cambridge.

We had a nice call from Mr. Watson some ten days ago.

We are getting along nicely with our work and have some good things for publication. Among them two new genera, one of which I expect to name for Coulter & the other for Brandegee.

You have only a surely named for you?
You must have a gesunar some day.

When do you expect to leave for the summer. We [hope] to see you before you go away. I will write you later on about our coming.

Yours truly
J W [---]

Washington D.C.
May 22/90

My dear Dean:

That Oak was not sent out from our Department.

Quercus pyramidalis is an English Oak. And is nearly a garden species. It is generally considered a variety of *Q. Robur*. It is a handsome tree in our location resembling the Lombardy Poplar.

Canby was down yesterday and spent the day with me.

The Dep. will probably want me to go early in June.

Resp'tly
J. N. Rose
Assist Botanist

Washington D.C.
Oct. 15th 1897

My dear Dean:

I know you will pardon my long delay when I tell you I am all alone, Dr Vasey being in the west & Coville on a wedding journey. Beside official work in great abundance I have charge of 12 clerks & Assistants which keep on a strain all the time. I return a part of your list today & will send the others shortly. I also send you a few good things now but hope to send you more later on.

If you do not get "The Grasses of the South West" Bull. no 12 inside of a week let me know. It is a beauty.

I am reading the last proof for Cont. No 3. It will soon be out

"Leclairs Coutinella".

Mr. Watson Compliments was much appreciated, but I am sorry it was not clearer.

This is the way our friend Shortburg's possessions are described by one of his western friends "He has a post office, a drug store, a lamp post, a wife & a daughter."

Yours truly
J. R. Rose

Washington
Jan. 18th 1862

My dear Dean!

You are no doubt
wroth with me for neglecting
you. I have been overworked is
my only excuse. I often think
of you and of your wants &c
but I am down in my office
now and do not get to see anything
else. Our collection is full of good
things if I could only get at them.
You might send down a
bundle!! to ___ ___ ____
to satisfy Dewey and ___ ___
that he gets your ___ installment.

We were old sorry to hear
that Mr. Hitson has been so
sick.

I sent you yesterday by your father the Fern Book I promised so long ago; if you do not get it please let me know.

Dr. Vasey feels pretty well. He will soon have out the 1st Vol. of his Manual on Grasses.

The Children are growing nicely. I mean to send you their pictures one of these days.

Call on me when you need my thing.

When you are at the gardens read Mush's review of Greene's Pittonia in the last Doc. It is rich.

With kindest regards I am always your friend

C. F. Cox

Washington D.C.
Oct. 13th 1892

My dear Deane:

At last I have time to answer your letter of Sept 7 although I believe I promised you one early in August. But I am not going to apologize now for this and yet perhaps I ought to for the postal card I sent during the summer for you misunderstood it. There has been no recent increase in my family except my botanical one. In the latter which is growing pretty fast & I am expecting some bloms and tripets soon. Now it was one of these plants "that I spoke of as a "pet without a name". One that I have been growing in my own yard all summer and watching with a good deal of interest. I had intended to follow up my card with a letter in a few days explaining the former. The plant is a very curious little Acantaceae for which I cannot find a generic place. I propose to name it for a particular friend of mine in my next "Contribution". I have it in flower and shall have made a fine plate to accompany the description.

My wife and family have been home about 2 weeks, and it is very nice to have them back again. I have made two visits to Indiana during the summer and will probably go again in a few weeks.

How I do wish you might make us a little visit this fall. Why can't you? We have received 5000 specimens this year and you can have your pick. But if you can't come I want you to do up a bundle of say 50 of your duplicates and send on your desiderata & I will see that some of your gaps are filled up. I want you to send a few duplicates so that I may have an excuse to get you out a bit.

I send you the pictures of my two babes. They are not very good but they are some of my own work.

How are things getting on at the herbarium? I would so much like to come up again.

Dr Vasey has just returned from Europe. He has been away about 6 weeks.

I will send you new labels for those tumbelifmae. I was so busy that I had to leave the labeling of my plants to one of the clerks and one who is very careless.

I mean to write again soon. Mrs Rose sends regards.

Yours very truly
J. N. Rose

U. S. DEPARTMENT OF AGRICULTURE,
DIVISION OF BOTANY,
WASHINGTON, D. C.

October 9th, 1894.

Mr. Walter Deane,
    Brewster Place, Cambridge, Mass.

My dear Deane:

    Your card of October 5th and package of AEgopodium were received yesterday. I thank you very much indeed for such a fine specimen. Even this plant has fairly good fruit. I am sorry your brother made the mistake. I have just had a similar experience. Sometime in the forties Sir William Hooker described <u>Angelica verticillata</u> from specimens sent from the Nez Perces Indian reservation in northern Idaho. Since then we have known nothing about the plant and Dr. Watson and others have thrown doubt upon its being an Angelica but could not suggest the proper genus. I have recently been looking the matter up and came to the conclusion that it was a Ligusticum. To a friend of mine who was just starting for the Nez Perces Indian reservation I gave a description and asked him to get specimens. A few days ago I received a specimen from him which turned out to be nothing but <u>Cicuta maculata</u>!

    Very sincerely yours,

    J N Rose

FMV

SMITHSONIAN INSTITUTION

S. P. LANGLEY, Secretary
G. BROWN GOODE, Assistant Secretary,
  In charge of U. S. National Museum

UNITED STATES NATIONAL MUSEUM

Washington, D.C., November 1, 1894

Mr. Walter Deane,

    Cambridge, Massachusetts.

My dear Mr. Deane:-

        Your letter of October 30, has just been received. I am sorry that you have not yet received Mr. Smith's paper on "Peach Yellows", but I will look the matter up in a day or two. The second part of Dr. Vasey's Grasses of the United States and British America has not yet been printed. Vol.3, No.2 is Prof. Coulter's paper on Cactaceae, which I suppose you have. No.8 of Vol.I is the last number of these volumes that has been issued. I think you have all the Contr. Nat. Herb. Did you ever receive the species of <u>Capsella draba</u> which I sent you just before you left for the summer? We have the herbarium about in shape now, but can only get the exogens and the endogens up to the grasses in our present quarters. The grasses, ferns, conifers and cryptogams still remain at the Department of Agriculture.

    I have just received my appointment this morning as "Assistant Curator in the Department of Botany" signed by Secretary Langley.

This is the first letter that I have signed with my new title.

Yours very truly,

J. N. Rose
Assistant Curator.

UNITED STATES DEPARTMENT OF AGRICULTURE,
DIVISION OF BOTANY,
WASHINGTON, D. C.

February 12, 1895.

Mr. Walter Deane,
    Cambridge, Mass.

My dear Mr. Deane:-

    I inclose several U.S. Department of Agriculture franks. The one which you inclose would have brought the package safely here. We occasionally have plants come in with franks several administrations old, but of course it is better to use the new ones. We have also Museum franks which I sometimes use, but they cause me more trouble than the other kind.

    I suppose you have received my new Contributions by this time.

          Yours very truly,

          Assistant Botanist.

UNITED STATES DEPARTMENT OF AGRICULTURE,
DIVISION OF BOTANY,
WASHINGTON, D. C.

February 19, 1895.

Mr. Walter Deane,
    Cambridge, Mass.

My dear Mr. Deane:-

Your specimen of so called Thaspium aureum has been received and returned. It is as you guessed, good Zizia aurea. I have a letter this morning from Mr. Pollock of Buckhannon, West Virginia. In answer to my letter regarding his Thaspium aureum, he says he is also in receipt of a letter from you expressing doubt regarding his species. No, I do not have a copy of "Natural Science and Religion" but would be very glad to receive a copy. *You may find it if you wish.* I do not understand why you have not received a copy of my Contribution No. 9. If it has not reached you by this time please send me a line and I will see that you are supplied at once. I have sent you a specimen of Tradescantia virginica var. villosa Watson. Commelina communis is very common about Washington and I will try and get you a good specimen of it this coming season. This is the plant that Dr. Morong referred to in the Torrey Bulletin Vol. XX, p. 469.

                                        Yours very truly, J. N. Rose
                                            Assistant Botanist.

V
Personal.

UNITED STATES DEPARTMENT OF AGRICULTURE,
DIVISION OF BOTANY,
WASHINGTON, D. C.

March 13, 1895.

Mr. Walter Deane,

#5 Brewster Place,

Cambridge, Massachusetts.

My dear Deane:-

I received your little volume containing Dr. Gray's lectures on "Natural Science and Religion." I have been looking over it and find it a most delightful little book. I hope to return it to you shortly, although my wife's sickness prevents my doing very much reading at home. I have laid aside for you good fruiting specimens of the two species of Cymopterus which comes in your region. I inclose a letter of Dr. Palmer's which you are to keep for your collection. Also one of Dr. Hasse's, Mrs Brandegee's, one of President Coulter's brother's and of Walter H. Evans who monographed Cornus. You may not care for some of these and if so you may return them when writing again. I have looked over the Myosotis puzzle. I think Prof. Ward must be wrong in calling his specimen . arvensis although specimens of Mr. Coville also from the District and one of Mr. Bush's from the Indian Territory are so labeled. They are all much nearer .verna and I see no reason except that the longer calyx teeth are hardly twice as long as the shorter, to keep it out of the var. macrosperma. I have labeled our specimens in this way as this appears to be the best thing to do.

Professor Coulter spent a week with me the last part of February and I can assure you that we put in considerable work upon Umbelliferae. Besides a score of new species we have about decided upon three new genera. The one you will probably be most interested in is Deanea, standing on two legs, D.tuberosa and D.nudicaulis I am glad that Deanea is to be such a near relative of Coulterophytum and Rhodosciadium.

No, I have not yet seen Bailey's Field and Garden Botany, although we have an order in for it.

Yours truly,

J.N. Rose

V

UNITED STATES DEPARTMENT OF AGRICULTURE,
DIVISION OF BOTANY,
WASHINGTON, D. C.

March 20, 1895.

Mr. Walter Deane,

    Cambridge, Mass.

My dear Mr. Deane:-

    Your note of recent date has been received. Our new genus Deanea I think is going to be able to stand, but I purpose to give it one more careful going over before publishing it. I feel quite disappointed that I will not be able to have it illustrated here. I had planned to figure it in our Contributions and had kept it back till the very last. Mr. Coville, however, had a plant which he was anxious to have figured and this consequently cut Deanea out. Have you not a good friend at Cambridge who would be willing to assume the expens of a plate? Mr. Faxton and Meisel could be depended upon to make an elegant plate. I think there would be no trouble then in getting the genus published in the Botanical Gazette. You are not to understand that I wish you to be at any personal expense in this matter, but this is simply a suggestion that you might be able to carry out. There is a chance yet of my having an illustration made here and if so I shall most certainly avail myself of it. There is a very good reason for the

WD2

genus Deanea. Genera are not named in the same way as species. Our brief note as to why we named the genus cannot be disputed by any one.

I send you to-day the two specimens of Cymopterus. I think you will be pleased with them.

Yours very truly,

J N Rose

Assistant Botanist.

UNITED STATES DEPARTMENT OF AGRICULTURE,
DIVISION OF BOTANY,
WASHINGTON, D. C.

July 19, 1895.

Mr. Walter Deane,
   Whitefield, N.H.

My dear Deane:-

Hurrah for Deanea! She is a beauty! I have just received Meisel's proof from Faxon and I am very much pleased with it, and I think you will be also. The plate is No.27, and I suppose will be out soon, although it does not seem to be promised for next month. No, no, I never intended to imply that I considered my correspondence with regard to the plate as any trouble at all, I **really** enjoyed doing something of this kind for you. I suppose you have seen the last Gazette. As you do not get the Journal of Botany I inclose a copy of one of the articles which I think you will appreciate.

Yours very truly,

J. N. Rose

I am sorry about the mistake in the address but I leave those things to my clerk. They ought not to occur. My family are doing nicely. I shall spend September with them. My kind regards to Mrs Deane. What did you think of Lovell's latest?

J.N.R.

UNITED STATES DEPARTMENT OF AGRICULTURE,
DIVISION OF BOTANY,
WASHINGTON, D. C.

July 25, 1895.

Mr. Walter Deane,

    Cambridge, Mass.

My dear Deane:-

    Your letter of July 22d is at hand. I fear the illustration of <u>Deanea</u> is going to prove an expensive luxury to you. You ought to have written to me again about the matter. Indeed, I should have considered it no bother at all. I feel that I have been well paid for any trouble that I have been put to. I marked on the MS. for 60 separates, as I knew the Gazette did not print extras unless so indicated on the MS. 50 I intended for you and 10 for myself. I ordered 450 plates, on Mr. Faxon's statement that the Gazette would require 400. I only want a few copies, certainly not more than 10 as nearly all my botanical correspondents receive the Gazette. I think that if I were in your place, I would recall your order on Meisel until you hear definitely from Barnes as to the number of plates they will actually need. I do not think that you ought to go to the additional expense. I intend to as ask Mr. Coville today to have the plate reissued in our Contributions. I doubt, however, whether this can be done.

WD2

The article in the Journal of Botany came out in the July number. As you see I am still in Washington and it is very doubtful whether I shall get away on any official business. By the way have you a photograph of J.W. Short? When he dies he left his entire herbarium to the Smithsonian Institution, but for some reason it never came here. I came upon this information rather incidentally, and have been looking up the matter since. I find in a letter written to Dr. Gray in 1883 the following clause from his will.

"I give and bequeath my herbarium of dried plants to the Smithsonian Institution of Washington City, upon the condition that the collection be carefully preserved and subject at all times to the inspection of those in pursuit of botanical knowledge."

When you get back to Cambridge I may ask you to look up some of his correspondence with Dr. Gray.

Yours very truly,

J.N. Rose

Since dictating the above I have had a talk with Coville. He is much pleased with the plate of Deanea and has agreed to have it reissued. The plate is a little large for our use and so we must use the photo process. Really I don't think you need get so many copies of your paper. I can get along with a half dozen for we will have 2500 here. You will have plenty of time to write to Barnes & Russel.

(over)

I miss the wife & babe. The little babe has learned to stand since going away. My wife has been much better this summer. Since writing the above I find I have a chance of doing some fieldwork and may see my family next week. My kind regards to Mrs Deane. Mrs Rose always wants to read your letters too. She expects me to send your letters along promptly with mine. It is very foolish in me but I write every day!

 I shall write soon again

    J N Rose

U. S. NATIONAL MUSEUM
WASHINGTON CITY

Dec.5,1895.

Mr.Walter Deane,
            Cambridge, Mass.
My dear Mr.Deane:-

            Your card and note of recent date were duly received. I have asked that a copy of the Agricultural Report be sent you and you have doubtless received it before this time. With regard to Mrs.Gray's questions, I would state that I was born, at least so I have been told, near Liberty, in Union Co., Indiana, January 11,1862. Dr.Watson named the genus Rhodosciadium (Proc. Amer. Acad. 25: 151,1890) for me. As L.H.Bailey has said, it was rather an obscure compliment.

The Smithsonian Institution are preparing a Semi-Centennial book and have just been to see me about some data for a sketch to appear there.

        Yours very truly,

        J. N. Rose

U. S. DEPARTMENT OF AGRICULTURE,
DIVISION OF BOTANY,
WASHINGTON, D. C.

January 14, 1896.

Mr. Walter Deane,

    Cambridge, Mass.

My dear Mr. Deane:-

    I return to you to-day your Thaspium collected by Mr. Pollock, as well as the Zizia which I seem to have had on hand some time. The Zizia is distinguished from the Thaspium chiefly by the fruit not being winged and the central fruit in the umbel being sessile. I do not think there is more than one species of the Thaspium aureum group and if so, it is a little hard to say what name should be used. I have not been able to take up the question since I wrote to you and I really have no new information to send you.

    I send you also a few additional specimens, some of which may be of use to you.

    Professor Wheeler is now at work in the herbarium and will be here several weeks.

    I also send you a set of my photographs which you may wish to put in your herbarium.

                                  Yours very truly,

                                  J. N. Rose

                                  Assistant Botanist.

V

U. S. DEPARTMENT OF AGRICULTURE,
DIVISION OF BOTANY,
WASHINGTON, D. C.

February 11, 1896.

Mr. Walter Deane,
    Cambridge, Mass.

My dear Mr. Deane:-

    I have forgotten whether I told you that the plant you sent me from West Virginia was a Thaspium, probably T. trifoliatum.

                Yours very respectfully,

                      Assistant Botanist.

U. S. DEPARTMENT OF AGRICULTURE,
DIVISION OF BOTANY,
WASHINGTON, D. C.

March 13, 1896.

Mr. Walter Deane,

Cambridge, Mass.

My dear Deane:-

      The engraving of Dr. Gray reached me last enening and appears to be in perfectly good condition. I will take the best of care of it and return it directly to you at the close of the Exhibition. How I wish you were to be here! I find that the "Bee Bulletin" is entirely exhausted. A bill has just passed the House, however, authorizing the printing of 20,000 copies! I have sent your address to the author of the bulletin and he promises to see that you get a copy if the bill becomes a law. You had better let me send your brother a copy also.

                              Yours very truly,

P.S. I do not quite understand when you say Heracleum lanatum has two tubes on the commissural and 4 in the intervals. You do not mean of course, 4 in each interval; there are 4 intervals on the back and therefore the oil tubes would be solitary, and so we say under 2* on page 18. If this is not the plan of your fruit then you have something which I have never seen. By the way, I have just got hold of a photograph of this species from Commarder Islands Would you like to have one for your herbarium?

U. S. DEPARTMENT OF AGRICULTURE,
DIVISION OF BOTANY,
WASHINGTON, D. C.

March 28,1896.

Mr. Walter Deane,

    Cambridge, Mass.

My dear Deane:-

    I should have answered your letter of March 15th before this, but I have been expecting a line from you every day regarding the disposal of Dr. Gray's picture. I think the Smithsonian Institution would be glad to get the picture, although Professor Goode seemed to think that they had one. The matter came up incidently, and if you wish I will find out definitely with regard to it.

    The Exhibition was quite a success, there being some 700 pictures on exhibition of which perhaps 35 were botanists.

    A new 20,000 edition of the "Bee book" has been ordered and I will see that both you and your brother get a copy.

    I am glad to hear about your "Park Flora." I hope you will be able to send me a copy when completed.

    I shall not return the photograph until I hear from you.

                     Yours very truly,

                         J.N.Rose

U. S. DEPARTMENT OF AGRICULTURE,
DIVISION OF BOTANY,
WASHINGTON, D. C.

April 10, 1896.

Mr. Walter Deane,

　　Cambridge, Mass;

My dear Deane:-

　　　　Your postal card of April 2d. was duly received. <u>Verbascum phlomoides</u> is firmly established at Dickey's Mills, Ky., and threatens to prove a very troublesome weed.

　　<u>Hymenocallis occidentalis</u> is the plant referred to in Gray's Manual, and grows naturally about Litchfield, Kentucky.

　　　　　　　　　　　　Yours very truly,

　　　　　　　　　　　　　　Assistant Botanist.

U. S. DEPARTMENT OF AGRICULTURE,

DIVISION OF BOTANY,

WASHINGTON, D. C.

June 3, 1898.

Mr. Walter Deane;

    Cambridge, Mass.

My dear Deane:-

          I have just received your "Flora" prepared for the Metropolitan Park Commission. I am very much pleased with it. The only correction which I should make is that your name should appear upon the title page. The three accompanying maps will be helpful.

    I made a flying trip to Indiana 10 days ago. I send you to-day a short paper on <u>Tradescantia micrantha</u> etc.

                      Yours very truly,

                            JNRose

I received quite an ovation while at home. My family are all quite well especially my wife. We have made no definite plans for the summer. I will have a short paper out in the Contributions in a few weeks with two drawings by Faxon one of Leibergia + the other of Roseanthus. Have had to change bogmans reference for myself. Of course I could not let it go just as he wrote it. Our kindest regards to Mrs Deane

                          Yours JNRose

U. S. DEPARTMENT OF AGRICULTURE,
DIVISION OF BOTANY,
WASHINGTON, D. C.

July 1, 1896.

Mr. Walter Deane,

   Cambridge, Mass.

My dear Deane:-

     Your kind letter of July 7th. has been received. I suppose you are now in the country enjoying your well earned vacation. I will soon have out another short paper of which page proof has just been read.

   Have you received a copy of the year book of the Department of Agriculture for 1895? It is just out and has considerable botany in it.

   I still have your list of Umbellifer desiderata, but I am sorry to say that very little in your line is coming in.

               Yours very truly,

                 J. N. Rose

I am now over to the museum for good, having just given up my place in the Agr. Dept. to accept a like place in the Nat. museum. The herbarium is now entirely under the care of the Smithsonian. They have $10,000 for our work and get going for clerk hire. They will have about $1000 to put on plants. They have added 60,000 sheets to the collection since I moved over here so months ago.

My family are well except baby Martha. She has been quite [sick] for 10 days past and under the Doc. Care. She is a little better now. Her little red ball which she loved so much is still whole but the gas in now all out and Jeouse is as limp as a rag.

We expect a house full of friends next week. I wish I could get up to Cambridge this summer but probaly shall not,

Give our kind regards to Mrs Dean

Your friend

J. W. Rose

My dear Deane:

I have just learned this moment that I can go to Cambridge next month. Don't ask me for details for I can not give them now! My boy never looked forward to Christmas with more pleasure.

Will try and write tomorrow

J M Rose

SMITHSONIAN INSTITUTION

UNITED STATES NATIONAL MUSEUM

S. P. LANGLEY, Secretary
G. BROWN GOODE, Assistant Secretary,
In charge of U. S. National Museum.

Washington, D.C., August 18, 1896.

Mr. Walter Deane,

    Jaffrey, N.H.

My dear Deane:-

    Your letters of recent date have both been received as well as one of much older date. I have been in the city all summer hard at work and being short of help, letter writing of all kinds has been neglected.

    I am glad you are pleased with Roseanthus, and of course I am. Paxton's plate is good and best of all is accurate. I thank you very much for your kind words and I appreciate them very much coming from you.

    You will be pleased to hear that I am just now sending an order to Mr. Faxon for 12 new plates to accompany a paper which I am almost ready to publish upon. I am very much encouraged by the spirit in which my work and recommendations are received by the authorities.

    Of course your plant is Angelica hirsuta. The calyx lobes are small but hardly prominent, certainly not obsolete. Of course the Manual should have had a modifying clause. Coulter and Rose say "Calyx teeth mostly obsolete," which must have referred to A. hirsuta. I have taken occasion to go over all our Angelica's (16 species) and have made the accompanying memorandum regarding them: Only two species, A. dentata and A. hirsuta have calyx teeth. I have never found that the calyx teeth amount to much in Umbelliferae, yet in cases like this the fact should be stated under the species, as it may be separated by this alone.

                                  Yours very truly,

                                  J N Rose

                                Assistant Curator,

                                Department of Botany.

Angelica.

A. arguta   Calyx teeth wanting.

A. attropurpurea   Calyx teeth wanting.

A. Breweri   Calyx teeth wanting.

A. Canbyi   Calyx teeth wanting.

A. Curtisii   Calyx teeth wanting.

A. Dawsonii   Calyx teeth wanting.

A. dentata   Calyx teeth small.

A. genuflexa   Calyx teeth wanting.

A. Hendersoni   Calyx teeth wanting.

A. hirsuta   Calyx teeth small.

A. leporina   Calyx teeth wanting.

A. lineariloba   Calyx teeth wanting.

A. lyallii   Calyx teeth wanting.

A. pinnata   Calyx teeth wanting.

A. tomentosa   Calyx teeth wanting.

A. Wheeleri   Calyx teeth wanting.

Washington, D.C., August 22, 1896.

Mr. Walter Deane,
    Jeffrey, New Hampshire.
My dear Deane:-

Your two cards at hand. I had not written you regarding my plans as they are still a little uncertain.
My family will leave for Indiana soon after the 1st. but I shall remain here perhaps a week when I shall proceed to Cambridge, stopping perhaps both at Philadelphia and New York City. If possible I shall delay my visit so as to spend at least one week of October at Cambridge, although I cannot tell definitely until I receive my instructions.

My papers have just arrived. They state that my work must be done during September in which case, I shall miss you. I shall be dreadfully sorry if such shall be the case. If I can I shall have the date changed.

My family are unusually well. Little Martha was very sick for nearly a month but is again quite like herself. Joseph Jr. is growing into quite a manly little fellow. He is seven next week. He has not been in school quite 6 months but will enter third grade this fall. Rebecca is our darling, at least one of them. Have I told you what a fine little thing she is? She is very fond of Bible stories & Uncle Ott likes most the beheading of John the Baptist.

Mrs Rose is getting along nicely. I hope the trip west will do her good. I will spend October with Lesa and stay until after the election.

I will send you one of my papers but am waiting until I get my sovens.

Velo foke I may see you. I will write again soon.

My kind regards to Mrs Deane.

Your friend.
J. M. Rose

SMITHSONIAN INSTITUTION

Z.

S. P. LANGLEY, Secretary
G. BROWN GOODE, Assistant Secretary,
In charge of U. S. National Museum

UNITED STATES NATIONAL MUSEUM

Washington, D.C., September 1, 1896.

Mr. Walter Deane,

Jaffrey, New Hampshire.

My dear Deane:

I felt very much disappointed when I learned that you would not be home until October and that the wording of my authorization would require that my visit be made in September. I have been quite puzzled how to get around the technical wording of my instructions which only needed the addition of a single word to allow me to do just what I wanted; but no one could make the change except the Secretary, and yet I hesitated to bother him unless I had a very good excuse. I finally managed to get courage to ask for a change which was readily granted. My plan now is to leave here the last of next week, and will reach Cambridge early the following week. I do not know just how long I can remain but I hope until after you are back at Cambridge.

My family leave for Indiana, Thursday of this week.

I shall spend a day or two in Philadelphia on my way north. I am looking forward to a most enjoyable stay at the Herbarium.

I have just had a most cordial note from Dr. Robinson assuring me of a friendly welcome. I shall miss you of course. In the past I have always looked (and not in vain) for you on about the second day of my visit.

Yours very truly,

J. N. Rose

COSMOS CLUB,
WASHINGTON. D.C.

Oct 16/96

My dear Deane:

Your card & letter have been received. It was very good of you to write. I was very anxious to hear about the little girl. I was not surprised for you know there was very little hope on Saturday.

I did not get home until Wednesday night. Did not do much in New York. The collection is much smaller than the Gray in National Herb.

You do not have Trad. montana.

T. montana is near T. pilosa
See the figures of T. floridana
as to number of rud. It has 6 ands!
I have good news from
my family. I expect to join
them next week. I leave Wash
ington next Thursday. My
address will be Liberty Ind.

Tell Mrs Doane that the chocolate
pot came through without mishap.
Thanks to her care.

I send you two copies to-morrow.
There is no making for those
warm frug thermal refs to regaling
Song. Always call on me.

I often think of my pleas-nt
visit with you.
My kind regards to Mrs Deane
Your friend
[signature]

U. S. NATIONAL MUSEUM
WASHINGTON CITY

Jan - 1897.

My dear Mr. Crane:

You see I am making a good stand for the New Year. Of course I have not intended to leave your letter unanswered so long, but I have never been so busy. I have hardly been able to look over the work I did at Cambridge or to put it into shape for publication. I hope you are well. Our little friend Miss Gemmett has been home and just returned to Cambridge.

day of his [?] care.

It is a little more than a year since I announced the arrival of a pair of twins, now another one are here. You understand that these are both [?]eas and come from Mexico. I like to have one or both illustrated by [?] you very soon.

Our friend Theo Holm has made himself very unpopular here by his uncalled for criticism of his associates here. I may write to you of this again I suppose. You have seen the haec[?] mi[?]. Mrs Robinson is making for me.

[sideways text:]
hard, hope we may will this week, the children are unusually well although we have had to take Rebecca out of school on account of her cold.
Both the boss and I send kind regards.
Yours [?] [?]
[signature]

V

SMITHSONIAN INSTITUTION

S. P. LANGLEY, Secretary
G. BROWN GOODE, Assistant Secretary,
In charge of U. S. National Museum

UNITED STATES NATIONAL MUSEUM

Washington, D.C., Jan. 26, 1897.

Mr Walter Deane,

    Cambridge, Mass.

My dear Mr. Deane:-

    Your kind note was duly received and I shall try to answer it very soon. I wish to call your attention to several government publications in which you will be very much interested and if you have not received them I will be pleased to try and get them for you. The 1st. is the Report of the U.S. National Museum for 1894, 2d. a Cotton Bulletin by the Department of Agriculture 3d. a list of the Trees of the United States, by Mr. George B. Sudworth, 4th. The Russian Fur Seal Islands, by Dr. Stejneger. The latter contains an interesting picture of <u>Heracleum lanatum</u> as well as a short account of the Flora of these islands.

                Yours very truly,

                Assistant Curator,

                Department of Botany.

SONIAN INSTIT/

UNITED STATES NA

Washington, D.C., Feb.27,1897.

Mr.Walter Deane,

Cambridge,Mass.

My dear Mr.Deane:-

I suppose you have received all those books requested in your last postal card, except the Cotton Bulletin. I cannot get this for you until the new edition is ready. I think I sent you in addition the last report of the Secretary of the Smithsonian Institution.

Will you please look into your bundle of <u>Tiedmannia</u> at <u>T.teretifolia</u>. The specimen sent out by Mr.Canby from Ellendale, Delaware has very different fruit from the one which comes from Florida and thereabouts. My Delaware plant is without root or root leaves. Let me know what you find in your herbarium. When you are at the Gray herbarium next time will you look up the material there also? Do not make a special trip for I am in no hurry.

Yours very truly,

Assistant Curator,
Department of Botany.

SMITHSONIAN INSTITUTION

UNITED STATES NATIONAL MUSEUM

S. P. LANGLEY, Secretary
G. BROWN GOODE, Assistant Secretary,
   In charge of U. S. National Museum

Washington, D.C., March 8, 1897.

Mr. Walter Deane,

    Cambridge, Mass.

My dear Mr. Deane:-

    Your kind letter was duly received. I have been so very busy that I have scarcely had time for letters, in fact I have not been able to put my MS. in shape which I prepared in Cambridge last fall. So you see there is no need of my going back there for the present at least.

    I will have a note with an illustration of <u>Agava attenuata</u> in an early number of Garden and Forest and I have just finished an elegant plant of <u>Chrysosplenium</u> which is to appear in Mr. Macoun's list of the plants from the Pribilof Islands to be published in the Bering Sea Report. I will try to get you a copy. . I also send you a copy of a new <u>Tradescantia</u> which has just appeared in Hooker's Icones. When you are at the Garden again look at the plates in Hooker's Icones, Nos. 2504- 2511. Most of the material for these drawings was sent on by me. You will see that Hemsley makes a pleasant reference to it.

WD2

    I think I wrote to you some months ago that I was planning to name a new genus for Dr. Robinson, but it is a little hard to decide upon the name. <u>Robinsonia</u> is a very pretty name but of course this can not be used. The name is already long and can only take a short prefix or suffix. What would you think of <u>Neorobinsonia</u>? Would it be too much trouble for you to find out in a round about way what would be his wishes in the matter. My new genus contains 3 species of handsome flowering shrubs or trees from Mexico.

    The herbarium people have got things turned about with reference to <u>Zizia</u> and <u>Thaspium</u>. I transferred nearly all of their <u>Thaspium</u> <u>aureum</u> to <u>Zizia</u> when I was there in the fall. I think you have as good a representation of <u>Thaspium</u> <u>aureum</u> as any one in this country. I have seen Hills article but have not had time to read it.

                                            Yours very truly,

                                              Assistant Curator,

                                              Department of Botany.

SMITHSONIAN INSTITUTION

S. P. LANGLEY, Secretary
G. BROWN GOODE, Assistant Secretary,
in charge of U. S. National Museum

UNITED STATES NATIONAL MUSEUM

Washington, D.C., March 13, 1897.

Mr. Walter Deane,

    Cambridge, Mass.

My dear Deane:-

    Your kind notes of March 10th and 11th are at hand. I thank you very much for your trouble in looking up the Tiedemannia. All the carpels you send have the thin wings and prominent disk of the typical form. I think I must divide my material with you.

    Dr. Britton has been down for a day this week going over the Umbelliferae with me. I have told him what I thought about Thaspium and I am inclined to think that he will knock out T. aureum entirely leaving only Thaspium trifoliatum. I thank you very much for seeing Dr. Robinson about the new genus. I understand from your note that he would not object to the proposed name in any way.

    The two new Deaneaes are resting quietly on my table.

    I am expecting Professor Coulter the last of this month when we shall then put our notes in shape for printing. I hope to have drawings made of both species but I am not yet quite certain that it can be done.

                          Yours very truly,

                            F. McC——

                        Assistant Curator, Depart. of Botany.

SMITHSONIAN INSTITUTION

S. P. LANGLEY, Secretary
G. BROWN GOODE, Assistant Secretary,
in charge of U. S. National Museum

UNITED STATES NATIONAL MUSEUM

Washington, D.C., April 6, 1897.

Mr. Walter Deane,

    Cambridge, Mass.

My dear Deane:-

    Robinsonella it shall be! I should have written and thanked you for your kindness but I have been devoting every minute to Umbelliferae work, Professor Coulter having come on for a short visit. We have outlined a great deal of work including three new species of Deanea.

    I have just received Mrs. Robinson's tracings with which I am exceedingly well pleased.

    Of course you are right about the orchid leaves, as you usually are. I certainly had in mind leaves like Habenaria orbiculata and I am sorry to have made this slip. Still they may be called an orchid-like leaves.

    The remark in my last letter that "I understood Dr. Robinson did not object to the new genus" was intended as a question. You had stated in your card of the day before that you had spoken to Dr. Robinson about the genus, but wrote nothing else. I infered that it was agreeable and that you were too busy to write farther.

Can you send me a fruit or two from each of your specimens of Crantzia.. See if all your eastern ones have peduncles longer than the leaves.

I have a little paper on the genus Chrysosplenium in the April Gazette.

Yours very truly,

Assistant Curator,
Department of Botany.

SMITHSONIAN INSTITUTION

UNITED STATES NATIONAL MUSEUM

S. P. LANGLEY, Secretary
G. BROWN GOODE, Assistant Secretary,
In charge of U. S. National Museum

Washington, D.C., April 15. 1897.

Mr. Walter Deane,

    Cambridge, Mass.

My dear Deane:-

    I thank you very much for your promptness in sending me the fruits of <u>Crantzia</u>. I was disappointed to find that there was not a better representation in your model herbarium. Perhaps this coming season we may be able to obtain a good supply of fruiting specimens. We think we can recognize four well marked species of this genus in the United States. One western, one inland, one along the Atlantic Coast from Massachusetts to Mississippi, while the fourth is found only in one locality in North Carolina. I inclose a carpel of the latter. Note the peculiar ribbing to the fruit.

    I am delighted to hear that you are to have such congenial work for the coming season. I trust, however, that you will not be

Acaponeta, Mex.
July 31/1897

My dear Deane:

Here is my trip without the trimmings.

I left home on May the 27 for St Louis via Libsey Ind; spent one day at the Shaw Gardens. At Poplar Grove Mo. I found that Dr. Palmer was on the train and he came on as far as Mazatlan with me. As we neared El Paso I met Mr. C. G. Pringle who had been on the train for 24 hours! It was very amusing but I cannot tell of our meeting now. We spent two days together at El Paso collecting both in Mexico & on Mt Franklin. Tex.

Then on to Guaymas via Benson Ariz.
Ten days or so were spent here, and I collected many specimens from the very plants from which Dr. Watson's type specimens came! Good Dr. Palmer pointed out as I collected the specimens just where his were taken! Then too I saw that curious tree which bears Dr. Watson's name. You remember it in the Contributions? One tree was growing in a yard just before a window. How I should like to have it in my yard.
On June the 12 I left Guaymas for Mazatlan via La Paz & Altata. A stop of one day was made at each place and collecting was done of course. Cacti Agaves etc were taken to be sent back alive. From Mazatlan I came by stage to this place 150 miles away. It was made at night, a stop of one day being made at Rosario. At Acaponeta I joined Mr Nelson & Goldman and have been with them ever since.

I spent 12 days here, then back to Rosario via Esquinapan. Several days were spent at Rosario. Then a ten days trip was made up into the Mts. to the east via Tamarindo, Matatan Palmareta Colomos to near Palomosas. You will only find the latter place on your map. 200 species were brought back; 5 oaks, 2 pines, 2 palms, 2 tree Ipomeas, wild potatoes, 4 species of Prionosciadium — but think of it 3 are only in leaf; etc etc.; then back to Rosario, Esquinapan, Concepcion & at last here at Acaponeta again. My collection is growing rapidly. I am getting bulbs and cacti agaves and ethnobotanical material outside of my sets of which I am making three. One is to stay at the National Herbarium one, to Kew and one of course to Harvard which shall be No. two. I must get some new species but I am especially anxious to get the old ones. If we can only get these gaps filled up in our collections then we can begin to name the many new species which Dr Palmer & Mr Pringle are bringing in each year. By the way I did not tell you I had the pleasure of introducing these two men who have both done so much work in Mexico but whose fathers have never before crossed.

Tell Dr Robinson I am counting on his help with my plants. I ought to write but this is the only letter I have written except my reports to the Department & hasty notes to my wife. — Tomorrow we are off for the Into. again call my at the following places Huejuquilla Colotlan, Bolaños. Guadalajara City of Mexico &c. In great haste I am your friend
J. N. Rose

Bolanos, Mexico
Sept. 13, 1897

My dear Deane:

Here we are at Bolanos, the Mecca of my trip. This was once a flourishing city of 50,000 people but now with scarce 400. Here an English company obtained $11,000,000. of silver but it cost them $13,000,000. An American company bought the mines a few years ago and likewise spend much money here & left it.

They built a fine house 100 broad with great porches & rooms surrounded by a high stone walls. Here we are lodged with two delightful American gentlemen who live here all alone. These are the only Americans I have met since leaving Rosario.

In the thirties Seemann came up to Bolaños from Tepic but since then no botanist has been here. This is a delightful place for the botanist and had I come here first I fear this would have been the end of my trip. The town is in a deep cañon at the east base of the Sierra Madre. The flora is purely tropical. From my window I can see the tops of the Sierra Madre.

I wish I might tell you of my trip which has been a very profitable one but shall wait until I return home to do so. I have passed the 1700 mark. I have just had a note from Mr. Pringle who says I will get 1000 species 100 of which will be new. I may have 25 but not many more. But this was not the chief object of my trip.

I hope to join Mr P next week in Guadalajara and from thence go on to the city of Mexico. I shall be there only a short time for I ought to be at home now.

In haste your friend
C. N. Rose

My dear Deane:

We are delayed another day so I shall add a few lines more.

Now that you are a "bird man" I ought to have given you some bird notes. Mr. Nelson is making a grand collection. He now has 4700 birds from Mexico!

The only bird collecting I have done was to get a few feathers for my wife. As we came, two days ago I bought through Riquelance near the lagoon south the coast 4/9 [fam oz] of "Garza" plumes. Not many was it? You know their value. They were taken from 4 birds. Your wife will know them & their value if you tell her they were Egret plumes   and you would as Ardea candidissima. If you write to Mrs Rose again don't tell her what they are but say you have heard about what I had for her.

One need to collect plants with a fine toothed comb to get every things. I enclose a few samples.

As ever JMK.

Planters Hotel
American and European. Henry Weaver, Manager.
ABSOLUTELY FIRE-PROOF.

St Louis — Oct 1 – 1897

My dear Deane:

Here it is the first of October and I am still away from home. I could be there tonight but the children would be so disappointed not to be able to meet "papa" that I have stopped over here for the day so as to reach home tomorrow morning.

I shall spend the day with Prof. Trelease however and am expecting a good time.

I have heard no botanical news since spring and I shall expect to have a full account from you.

I trust you have received my note from Bolivar. I could not get a stamp in the town so it was sent to Galveston, 75 miles away.

American and European   *Henry Weaver, Manager*

Planters Hotel

ABSOLUTELY FIRE-PROOF.

St. Louis, _____ 189__

We had a delightful trip to the Pato, west of Bolaños. From B. we went to Guadalajara a distance of 168 miles in 4 days! Then I went on to the City of Mexico and from there here.

Tell Dr. Robinson that his Coulterophytum is very common and that it is a very distinct genus. Rhodosciadium of Dr. Watson is common too. The two grow side by side on many mountain slopes!

But I must close.
Your friend
J N Rose

I enclose this in an envelope of the Emery Hotel as I wish you to see it. The menu card is piece of paper.
R

SMITHSONIAN INSTITUTION

UNITED STATES NATIONAL MUSEUM

S. P. LANGLEY
  SECRETARY
CHAS. D. WALCOTT
  ACTING ASSISTANT SECRETARY
  IN CHARGE U. S. NATIONAL MUSEUM

WASHINGTON, D. C., Dec. 14, 189_7_

Mr. Walter Deane,

    Cambridge, Mass.

My dear Deane:

    Your note of December 12th, is at hand. I have been trying for two months to write to you and only yesterday I got out your old letter to answer it. I am quite well but oh, so very busy. I wish I could show you the collection I brought back now that it is almost all mounted. I will have about 2500 numbers and although it contains many common species yet there is an indefinite number of new ones, many more than I had expected. Last week I worked over five genera containing an aggregate of twelve species, ten of which were new! I have forty sheets of oaks, all in fine condition; 50 sheets of ferns which are to go to our good friend Davenport. I shall soon send on some material to Dr. Robinson and when you are there ask to see it. Of course the specimens are not like the ones you make. Remember that they were collected while I was making some twenty to twenty-five miles on horseback per day, that often they were carried in the portfolio all day long put into press by candle light, dried on the backs of mules and some of them packed for 600 miles over the mountains subject to daily rains.

I am preparing a rough sketch of my trip with the places visited to help the herbarium people in naming my collection. This is not quite ready but when finished I will send it on in your care. There need be no haste in delivering it.

One word as to Umbelliferae- You seem not to have read my last items on this family! (See Britton and Brown Vol.2,508,foot note. Thaspium trifoliatum is the name to be used for this group of species. I question whether aureum should be used at all, but if so it can be no more than a variety, but there is very poor ground even for that as you will see from Dr.Britton's characterization. Both forms of course should be included in your catalogue. T.barbinode, you will of course admit. I suppose both Zizia aurea and Zizia cordata will be included in your catalogue.

       Yours very truly,

       Assistant Curator,

       Department of Botany,

Form No. 44.

NIGHT MESSAGE.
THE WESTERN UNION TELEGRAPH COMPANY.
INCORPORATED
21,000 OFFICES IN AMERICA.   CABLE SERVICE TO ALL THE WORLD.

This Company TRANSMITS and DELIVERS messages only on conditions limiting its liability, which have been assented to by the sender of the following message.
Errors can be guarded against only by repeating a message back to the sending station for comparison, and the Company will not hold itself liable for errors or delays in transmission or delivery of Unrepeated Night Messages, sent at reduced rates, beyond a sum equal to ten times the amount paid for transmission; nor in any case when the claim is not presented in writing within thirty days after the message is filed with the Company for transmission.
This is an UNREPEATED NIGHT MESSAGE, and is delivered by request of the sender, under the conditions named above.

THOS. T. ECKERT, President and General Manager.

NUMBER 5 B   SENT BY Ba   REC'D BY BW   7 Paid nite   CHECK

RECEIVED at _____ Jan 8 1898
Dated Washington D C 7
To Mr Walter Deane
    5 Brewster Place

But he shall be called Walter Deane

Mrs J. N. Rose

Washington, D.C.
Jan 11th 1898

My dear Deane:

Yes indeed we have a fine boy but he is not to be called Walter as you say in your letter to Mrs Rice. We call him Walter Deane. Mrs Rice says to let the Deane that Rice too to share in the name. The dear little fellow has already made for himself a place — in the home nest. But loving him has not pushed any one else aside but on his account we seem to love the others all the more. No one loves him more than dear baby Martha. She goes wild when permitted to see him and begs that he may only stay for her. She calls him

"Walter Dean" and says he is her baby. I found her this morning singing to herself (without tune of course) "Dear papa, dear papa, take care of my baby, Walter Dean" over and over again.

Joseph & Rebecca, keep account of the number of times they have seen the little boy.

Walter Deane was born Jan 6th 9:04 P.M. He weighed 7 lbs. Indeed he is a nice boy, perhaps a little too red just now but his little mother thinks him handsome even now. His eyes are probably blue and he has a sweet little mouth. Indeed you can't help be ashamed of him, for by the time you see him he will be a little beauty.

A word about his mother. Of course she is weak but growing stronger each day and hopes to be able to sit up Sunday.

She was inclined to scold me for signing her name to the telegram, but as she was not really a party, but a leader in this deception I thought she ought to submit. Then too it would do to put the words of Elizabeth into Weymouth!

Of course— we knew he was to be a boy, and long ago had decided upon the name. Nearly four years ago Joseph & Rebecca wanted some little playmates and not having much to say about it began to pray for them. In about 6 months Rebecca's prayer was answered and she stopped praying but would thank God for her little sister each night. We watched to see what Joseph would do expecting of course he would stop claiming his prayer had been answered in fact. But the little fellow kept bravely on at his proffer for three long years with no signs of an answer. Some months ago his sister Martha was taught an evening prayer and she herself added Joseph's little prayer which was kept up until the little brother came!

You don't know how we all enjoyed the good letters you and Mr Deane sent on. Mrs Rose of course could not read them but her face showed that she enjoyed them. And the little wife wishes me to say also that just as soon as she is strong enough she will write to you both. This is the longest letter I have written since I came home — to any I know and as I look it over it seems too personal to.

But I must close now. I shall have more to tell you of our little Walter Deane no doubt.

We both send dearest love to yourself & Mrs Deane.

Your friend,
J. Rose

Washington D C
Jan 16th 1898

My dear Deane:-

Your good letter was received yesterday morning. My little family are quite well especially Walter Deane who is 10 days old today. He was born Jan. 6th. I mention this again as the date seems to have been given wrong in my last letter. Mrs. Rose is growing stronger each day. She expects to sit up an hour this afternoon but it will be two weeks before she can take up her usual home work again. She wants to write to both you and Mrs. Deane but of course can not for some time. You will understand the reason of the delay in answering your good letters.

Little Walter Deane is indeed a fine fellow. He now weighs 10 lbs, so you see he is growing a little. He is a very good baby; a stranger would hardly know we had a baby in the house. he is so good and quiet. Every one likes the name we have chosen. Yes we call him Walter Deane all the time and hope to use the two words as one.

But I must close—

Your friend

J. W. Rose

Washington DC
Jan 20 1898

My dear Deane(?)

Your good letter of Jan. 25th was promptly received. Little Watson(?) some still continues to grow having added a half pound to his little self the third week of his mundane existence. Now as to your question about a present for the little boy. Of course it is very good in you both to think of such a thing but really you ought not to do it. I have talked the matter over with my wife and she agrees with me. If you have really decided to give the little boy a present I am sure his mother would be pleased

...her with a mug or porringer.
I think she would vote porringer
is enough. it is hard for her to
make up her mind. Your aunt Mrs.
Deane does you think him as
I know she will satisfied.

Mrs. Rice is praying often for
each day. She hopes to get
down stairs tomorrow. She
hopes to answer Mrs. L's own
good letter before the end of
the week.
  I presume was so busy.
      Your friend
        M R Rice

My dear Deane:

You note is just at hand. Sorry my last letter has not yet reached you. Perhaps it is in one of your lovely snow drifts. What a storm you have had!

We too have had a touch of winter.

A friend remarked the other day that I named my children like I did my plants. Said I gave them a name and then wrote Rose after it.

I wrote you in my letter that little Notre Dame's mother would be pleased with either a porringer or mug — but that I would vote porringer. Indeed it is very good of you both to want to send something. But really you ought not to do it.

In haste,
Jno Rose

Nat Museum
Feb 3/98

Washington D.C.
Feb. 26 1898

My dear Jene;

I know you are thinking bad things about me for not writing but I have been so very busy and not very well either. Of course you received Ms Kores letter in which she acknowledged the receipt of that pretty little jacket.

You will be pleased to learn that our little Walter Deane is quite well. He is now more than 7 weeks old and weighs 14 lbs. You would be surprised to see how the little one is developing — he loves to have us talk to him and returns the sweetest little smiles. He is such a good boy and just as little trouble as any baby could be.

The other children are devoted to him as are in fact the entire family.

Mrs. Rose is quite well again. It seems good to see her around once more.

We are expecting a little visit from Mother Rose early in the spring. She wants to see her new grandson so she says.

Remember us both to Mrs Deane.

Your friend

J M Rose

Washington DC
March 21/1898

My dear Deane:

Your letter of March the 14th. was (duly) received. I really must confess that you have checkmated me. But truly my dear Deane you ought to have let pass that little ornithological question for it was only 35 cents. But if you must pay it that you must allow me to return the dollar. Send me stamps and I will return them to you one at a time and I will get even with you before we are through with it.

Walter Deane is a very bad boy tonight and for the first time in many a week his mother is obliged to take him up

You do not know how much care he is. If it was not that we really loved him so much we would box him up and express him to 29 Brewster Place at once. He cannot be out of our thoughts one moment when he is awake. If in the upper hall he will try to fall down stairs so as to climb up or if he is in the lower hall he will climb up only to fall down. And so it is in the rooms — he climbs up onto the chairs only to topple over onto the floor.

As to works on butterflies & moths if you will just send me your list I will gladly look them up for you.

How would you like to spend 3 months in Mexico — May to July — all expenses paid; itinerary, Zacatecas, Guadalajara, City of Mexico etc.

Yours very truly
J. T. Ford

Washington DC
March 31/78

My dear Deane!
 Your card of the 29th is at hand. I have asked both the Museum & Agr. Dept to take a copy of your little monthly and I have no doubt but they will do so. How soon will it begin.

I have not been well this winter nor am I very well now. Still I get out to my office every day. The children are unusually

He is such a good boy
th. she can go out now for
an entire evening. Mrs. Rose
declares he is our best baby.
I have neglected to thank
you for that beautiful porringer
which you and Mrs. Dame
were so good send him.
Indeed we like it very
much. You could not
have sent anything which
would have pleased Mrs. Rose
more.
Did I tell you that one
of my two sheets of Carax from
Mexico was new at death
so says L.H.B. Dr. Robinson
has 3 new Bromeliae, one
M. Rizei.

I have two Beaulaujolyanum, perhaps one of Princei etc.
Remember us both to Mrs Dame.
Your friend
J. H. Rose

Washington D.C.
May 6th /98

My dear Deane:

It has been so long since I wrote you last that I am almost ashamed to write; be assured however that I often think of you in not a day passes but what your name passes my lips many time.

I have been feeling much better the past month. Yes I think my trouble has been due to my long stay in the tropics.

I am sending you a little paper of mine which Prof. Trelease asked me to furnish for his report. I am greatly interested just now in the Agaves. I have just discovered a second new species in our

Botanic Garden.

I enclose the list of Deanes which you asked for.

My mother has not been to see as yet but we expect her early this month.

I have nothing but good news to report regarding my Walter Deane. You never saw a finer or better boy. He is 4 month old tonight. He sleeps not less than 20 hours each day, he has seven meals a day, a morning bath and an afternoon outing. The children are devoted to him while his dear mother thinks there never was such a baby — at least — not more than three others.

Where do you expect to spend the summer?

It is almost a year since I started for Mexico! I wish I was going again.

Did you received an order for your New England Botanical Journal.

But I must close.

Remember as both to Mrs Dame

Your friend.

J N Rose

List of species of Deanea.

1 Deanea tuberosa Coulter & Rose.

2 Deanea nudicaulis Coulter & Rose.

3 Deanea nelsoni Coulter & Rose ined.

4 Deanea nelsoni Coulter & Rose ined.

5 Deanea diffusa Rose ined.

6 Deanea montana Rose ined.

7 *Walter* Deane(a) Rose inlit.

My dear Dean:

It's a long time since I wrote you last, I know, but I shall not try to make any excuses. I suppose you are away, but if I send this note to Cambridge it will probably find you.

You will be surprised to hear that I am still in Columbia. As you know I have not been well all winter and thought I needed more exercise. Mr. ___ Roo came to my relief and gave me a ___ of Columbia.

By Jiminy, what a time has come and gone. She was here ___ weeks. It was hard for us to give her

P.S.
I find your letter of the 16th on my desk this morning.

Yes Miller first called my attention to the little Houstonia and has asked me to look the plant up for him. Anything which you send him will come to me. He says he will name the plant if I don't. I suppose [he] says he is no botanist and [because] he ought [that] botanical matters along. I shall be in no hurry about publishing it however as the literature ought to be gone over carefully. It seems to have already been noticed and figured although wrongly named — see Gray's Syn. Fl. reference to Bot. Mag. t. 2522.

My family will probably remain here all summer. They are much more comfortably off here than they would be in the country. Then too we do not like to be far away from a good doctor.

Remember us both to Mrs Deane.

Rose

up. We are delighted that you have new grandson and thinks [it is] a fine boy. He is a baby no longer for he has been out of baby clothes more than a month. He has been quite well all summer and although he is not growing much now still he is holding his own very well.

We have wanted to send you his photograph but have not yet succeeded in getting a good negative.

I may be in to Cambridge for the A.A.S. next month. I want to do some work at the Herbarium and may try and do [a little?] of the same work. I have been feeling so much better this summer.

Hoping you are having a good summer.

Yours [sincerely]
J. N. Rose

My dear Deane:

How I should like to be in Boston this week! Indeed it was quite a disappointment to me to give up the trip. I know you had a grand time at the banquet Tuesday night. I am anxiously awaiting your account.

I had a half hour's call from Mr. Grinnman Saturday. I was sorry to see so little of him. He had planned to have some of the Washington Botanists in for an evening to meet him.

I shall depend on you for necessary aid in the Ad. Mr Ward as well as effects — a number of the other Washington papers are to be in Boston but I should like to have your reviews as well.

I am still uncertain what to do with that little Houstonia. Hope your materials will throw some light on the matter.

I am glad you enjoyed the pictures. They did not please us very well but I thought you would like to see them. We hope to get a better one. Our little Walter Deane is indeed a great comfort to us. You never saw a better baby. He sleeps all the night not wakening until about six when he wants his bottle. He is learning to sit & hold his bottle which he can do quite well.

I am still hard at work on the Hopi Mexican collection. It is extremely rich and valuable both Lem. Pursh though much lighter upon Seemann's trip through the Sierra Madre as I have extracted some of his types which have not been extracted before & it is with sole on what two new Cactaceae are with most remarkable petals — Long ones with boiled like this. Best more of them another time.

Your friend
J N Rose

UNITED STATES NATIONAL MUSEUM
UNDER DIRECTION OF
THE SMITHSONIAN INSTITUTION
WASHINGTON

Oct. 24, 1895.

My dear Dean:

If you really knew what a fine boy I have you would certainly understand how hard it is to write at night. Indeed I do very little work at night outside of my family interests. Of course I must go over the children's lessons with them, hear of how many words they have missed during the day etc. etc. Mrs. Rose and I both seem to have a somewhat different idea as to what parental duties are from many of our neighbors. I think I know why so many seemingly good people have bad children and why many boys do not like to stay at home at night etc. The feel as though we cannot give to much of the right kind of attention to our little ones.

But a word as to the family: 1stly Walter Deane is the dearest boy you ever saw. Indeed he is a real beauty — the pride and the joy of every one in this household. Walter Deane is first last and always in our acts. Your name is taken in vain a hundred times a day. If your good wife was dropped down on our corner blind folded she would probaly have a nervous chill from what she heard. Such as "There goes Walter Deane" "Kiss me Walter Deane" "See how Walter Deane stands" "Walter Deane's my boy." But enough of this. But indeed he is a fine specimen of baby-hood and I only wish you could see him.

UNITED STATES NATIONAL MUSEUM
UNDER DIRECTION OF
THE SMITHSONIAN INSTITUTION
WASHINGTON

He crawls everywhere and is just beginning to pull himself up on his feet.

Secondly, my good wife is unusually well this winter although her home cares take up most of her time. She wishes me to say that she means to answer Mrs Dean's good letter.

Thirdly; Martha is our most original child. I think I told you about her play teacher, Miss Cochemo (her own name) who lived all last winter

ago. A few Sundays after this I thought I would see what progress she was making so I asked Martha "what did you sing today" and she promptly replied "Cop Cop the whisky shop" a song her brother Joseph had brought from the street. You see she is gaining much delicious training.

Lilly & Rily Joseph & Rebecca are both in school and doing very nicely indeed.

Bitty. As for myself I have never been so well and have never had a better chance to turn off good work. My Mexican experience has been a great service to me and my collection is rich in new species. I am just now revising the Suborder Agaveae. I have taken out Manfreda from Agave. I already have 18 species! I have revised Polianthes (the tuberose) and referred to it Bravoa. I collected 5 species of this genus myself 4 of which are new!

V

SMITHSONIAN INSTITUTION

UNITED STATES NATIONAL MUSEUM

S. P. LANGLEY
SECRETARY, SMITHSONIAN INSTITUTION

WASHINGTON, D. C., Nov. 1, 1898.

Mr. Walter Deane,

    Cambridge, Mass.

My dear Deane:

    I inclose a letter which I have just received from Baker partly because I want you to see what he thinks of some of my work and also that you may show it to Dr. Robinson as it brings up one or two points about which we have had some correspondence. He will also be interested in the discovery of a new Addinsonian name. It will be interesting to see what our reformers will do with it. I have rather sad news to tell you. Drude has referred the genus Deanea to Rhodossiadium. I do not think he is right in his conclusions and yet I am disappointed that he does not recognize the genus. The alliance of Deanea seems to me to be elsewhere. If the name is to be given up I should not refer the genus as he does. I believe this and Museniopsis are the only two genera of mine which he does not accept. Museniopsis he referred to Velaea, but

SMITHSONIAN INSTITUTION

UNITED STATES NATIONAL MUSEUM

S. P. LANGLEY
SECRETARY, SMITHSONIAN INSTITUTION

WASHINGTON, D. C.,

in his appendix he recedes from this view.

Yours very truly,

Assistant Curator,

Department of Botany.

My dear Deane:

I have been sick for 4 or 5 days, a part of the time I have been at home and the rest of the time should have been. I am better now. I suppose you have heard of the sad death of G. H. Hicks. I do not know that you had ever met him although he has been to Cambridge once or twice. He had charge of our seed collection here and was doing splendid work. He leaves a wife and two babies. Although the. has been married some 18 years his first child was not born until about three years ago.

Our little folks have had such a joyful Christmas time. I do not know how many Christmas trees they have been to see this last week. Walter Deane can hardly be said to have enjoyed Christmas as such but he certainly has a good time all the time. I never saw such a sunny baby. He is a constant joy to us all. He is almost ready to walk alone. I wish you could see him while he is still a little boy.

I am looking for Prof. Boutelier early in the year. He says he is coming on for a week or 10 days. He shall do a little Umbelliferae work. I shall

in his reference of the genus to Rhodoциadium.

Mr. J. G. Smith read a paper on two new NewEngland plants before one of our Botanical Clubs recently. I knew of your wants and so spoke a good word for you but Mr Smith said he only had one set which was to come to the National Herbarium.

How is your NewEngland Botanical Magazine coming on? I suppose your first number will soon be out.

(But I must close —.

Your friend
J. N. Rose

Jan. 1/1899

SMITHSONIAN INSTITUTION

UNITED STATES NATIONAL MUSEUM

S. P. LANGLEY
SECRETARY, SMITHSONIAN INSTITUTION

WASHINGTON, D. C., Jan. 4, 1899.

Mr. Walter Deane,
  Cambridge, Mass.

My dear Deane:

To my great joy Mr. J. G. Smith sends me a duplicate type specimen of Lophotocarpus spathulatus" for Mr. Walter Deane, whose address I do not know. I take great pleasure in forwarding this specimen to Mr. Deane. You may already have the species in your collection. Tell me what you think of it. Mr. Smith also has a new Sagittaria from New England but I fear I can not get a specimen for you. Mr. Smith's address is, Division of Agrostology, Department of Agriculture.

Yours very truly,

J. N. Rose

Assistant Curator,
  Department of Botany.

My dear Deane

We have enjoyed all your letters especially the one to your little namesake. You do not know what a household word your name has become at least in one home in Washington.

Little Walter Deane is very well indeed. He is so big that we have had to give up weighing him by hand. Although he still goes about the room fastest on all four yet he loves to push a chair ahead of him. He will soon however be walking alone for he is just gaining a little more confidence in himself.

You do not know how much care the dear little fellow is

just now. Nothing is safe— on tables unless it is out of his reach. But he is such a dear little boy that no one ever gets angry with him.

I think I wrote you that Prof. Coulter was coming on. The great storm came on just as he was to leave Chicago and his visit was given up for the present.

I am very busy with many kinds of work. Hope to have something ready for publication very soon.

A word about that spoon. I do not think I told you that I had it attended to. But I did at the very first opportunity. But it only cost a trifle so please do not think of this again.

I had such a nice call from Lloyd of Cincinnati; the older his heir, I believe he said he had not met you but that his brother was one of your warm friends. He is a most delightful man and I know you would enjoy him very much.

Please pardon my delay in not returning your Houstonia but I really do not know what to do with that mountain form.

What are you doing this winter? Mr. Applegate of Oregon who has been spending the winter at the herbarium has gone on to Cambridge for a week. He has collected largely in the north west.

Poor Mrs. Hicks has had to take a clerkship at $60.00 per month and leave her two babes with a servant! Isn't it sad.

But I must close

Your friend,
J M More

My dear Deane:

Yes I am off for Mexico again. I leave here May the 1st. and will be gone about 3 months. No I do not expect to undergo the exposure of my last trip but shall go this time in a palace car. I will visit all the large cities of Mexico making short trips of one or two days in length. I shall take Mr. Hough with me. I wish it was you. I have a fine chance to do some nice work, and I intend to do it.

Mrs. Rose will probably stay here.

Walter Deane has made great

proggress since I wrote to you last.

He has given up crawling altogether. He loves to climb up into the large chairs and now that he is able to get up and down from the chairs we can trust him more. For several weeks we had to keep most of our chairs turned upside down.

I can find no Government publication upon the butterflies.

I shall write again before it

Your friend,

J. M. Rose

UNITED STATES NATIONAL MUSEUM
UNDER DIRECTION OF
THE SMITHSONIAN INSTITUTION
WASHINGTON

City of Mexico
June 5th/1899

My dear Deane:

I found your good letter with two from my wife on my return to this city. I can assure you it was a very pleasant surprise. Indeed it was very good of you to write to me after I had neglected to tell you of my plans. The truth is I was too busy to write although I had planned to do so. Yes here I am again in Mexico - a country full of interest to the botanist. My plans this year is to see the country where other botanists have collected new species.

And these are my results so far.—
Between Lake Guzman & El Paso Dr
Parry collected Echinocactus Parryi. The
plant has not since been collected and
the type, [Phoeismu] has been lost. Mr. Pringle has looked
for it in vain. This year armed with a
description & figure Mr. Pringle & I again
looked for the plant and found it.

Then I went to Chihuahua City for
doubtful plants. Then to Aguas Calientes for
one of Hartweg's Mimosas and found it.

Then I went to the City of Mexico where
I have made my headquarters. Here I
have gone over much of Herr Bilbot Bourland's
ground, seen where Bourgeau, Hahn
and others have been and obtained
a far better understanding of the botanical
regions than I had before.

The in company with Mr Pringle
have crossed over the high mountains
at the south of the valley to Cuernavaca
This is along the old road leading
to Acapulco, and over which many
a botanist has passed, but where not

UNITED STATES NATIONAL MUSEUM
UNDER DIRECTION OF
THE SMITHSONIAN INSTITUTION
WASHINGTON

Mr. Pringle has especially done very much work. He seems to know every foot of ground. In making the journey we pass over miles of lava fields. From here many new species have come. It was delightful to have Mr. P. point out the very spot or bush from which some new species of mine had been taken. He would say — "There I got your last Dearea, here I found the plant which writes our names — Celastrus Pringlii Rose, etc." Then I went to Pachuca and Real del Monte where J. Coulter Humboldt and others have been.

I have also been to Jalapa in Vera Cruz where I spent a week. This is also famous as a botanical collecting ground. This is called the land of flowers. This briefly covers my trip so far although I have neglected to tell you much that has interested me especially of my trip to one of the great lakes here in the valley or how I obtained roots of a beautiful new water lily which grows there.

Mr. Pringle has gone home and very sorry I am to loose him.

Mrs. Rose's letters makes me home sick to see them all again. Little Walter Deane, she writes, looks like a big white ball. How I would love to see him. He's mother says however that he has entirely forgotten me. But I must close
Your friend
J.N.Rose

UNITED STATES NATIONAL MUSEUM
UNDER DIRECTION OF
THE SMITHSONIAN INSTITUTION
WASHINGTON

Puebla Mexico
June 28/1899

My dear Deane:

Since I wrote you last I have not been idle. I think I told you of my trip to Cuernavaca & Pachuca. I have since visited the ruins about Tula and a great pulque hacienda on the plains about Apam. I shall write a paper on this great drink of Mexico on my return and want to get as much information as possible first hand. Most Mexican travelers will tell you that the juice of the Agave changes into Pulque in two days while I find that the best pulque is often 25 days old! I am now on my way to the City of Mexico having been away 15 days on a trip to Oaxaca and the suburbs of Puebla. The trip to Oaxaca was grand but there was just enough danger in it to make me glad to be back from there. The road runs through great canons whose walls reach up hundreds of feet from the side of the track. During the rainy season the mountains become wet and slide down up on the track often cutting off the traffic for weeks. Even now the trains do not run at night. On our way down we were stopped three times by slides on the track. Oaxaca has been a great place for Botanical collectors and has been visited by Humboldt & Bonpland, Liebmann, Galeotti, Andrieux and more recently by Pringle & Nelson. It is also the home of Prof Conzatti and his very bright assistant Mr. Gonzalez. On the return trip I stopped off at Tomellin, and the Canon which runs up from the station.

UNITED STATES NATIONAL MUSEUM
UNDER DIRECTION OF
THE SMITHSONIAN INSTITUTION
WASHINGTON

And what a view we have of the mountains! Three great peaks reach up into the snow. To the east is beautiful Orizaba though now far away. When I was at Jalapa a month ago I was almost at its foot but the clouds hid the view. To the west was grand Popocatepetl and Ixtaccihuatl. I never before saw such great mountains. Other mountains nearly as grand as these are to be seen.

But it was the plant world which interested me most. I saw many of my own plants and it seemed like meeting old friends. Acacia Pringlei Rose only know to botanists from flowering specimens I saw in fruit. I found that the people here knew much better than I did. The firemen on the trains know it and glad to see it for it has great heat producing powers, the wood man knows it but avoids it because it is so very hard. But they don't know it as Acacia but as "Guebracho" (break ax). And so it was throughout my whole trip.

My work about Puebla has been most encouraging. I have recollected at or near the type several very old species which have given botanists much trouble. Liebmann visited Acatlan 50 or more years ago and collected several new plants. No one has been there since nor has his species been recollected. I had a great time in finding the place. I spent a day and walked 20 miles or more in my search. It is now only a small neglected hamlet of 10 to 12 houses.

On returning to Mexico I shall leave for Guadalajara & San Luis Potosi for a two weeks trip.

My wife has much to tell me of a big white baby who I should very much like to see but who has entirely forgotten me.

Your friend,
J. N. Rose

Liberty, Ind.
Aug 6th 1899

My dear Deane:

Your letter of Aug. 2 has been sent on here where I am spending a few quiet days with my family at my mother's home. I have been back from Mexico some 10 days. I shall write to you at length regarding my trip later on but just now I am trying to forget the last 2 months while I simply rest and get ready for a busy fall and winter for I have brought back a large collection with many interesting plants. I have only a few new species but I have some old ones which are much more interesting.

I found my family all quite well. Mrs. Rose was looking especially well and her long stay in the country has done her a world of good. The older children have run wild but have also grown strong and have been very happy at grandma Rose's. But none of them have changed more or look so well as dear little or rather big Walter Deane. For two or three days after I came home he refused to own me as his father. His mother calls him her little white lamb but he is more like a big white bull. He is just the dearest little fellow. You really must see him before long for he never will be as pretty again.

Mrs Rose has been having such a restful week. We go driving twice a day — either alone or with the children. Joseph and I go to the woods for flowers or to the creek for fossils and altogether we are having a good time. I shall not be in Washington before the first of September but the intervening time will be only too short.

I am glad you and Mrs. Dean are having such a good summer.

I shall write you you soon again.

Your friend
J. M. Rose

Liberty, Indiana
Aug. 18/99

My dear Deane:

Your good letter to me and your wife's to Mrs Rose have both been received, read and enjoyed. We are just home from a little outing. A week ago Wednesday we went to Peru, Indiana to visit a college classmate and a high school Mr. & Mrs. Dukes. They have a lovely home and surrounded by all the comforts that money will buy. We took the three older children and they had a most delightful time. From here we went to

Lafayette Indiana to visit my wife's Aunt & cousin. They live in a most beautiful home with lovely grounds and carriages and horses which we were free to use and enjoy. How the children did enjoy themselves as indeed we all did. This is the Aunt for whom our Martha is named. From here we went to Delphi to visit my wife's father and family. Our visits would have been all or more than we had hoped except for one unfortunate circumstance — we lost our trunk! We got it again the day after our return to Liberty.

I had a letter from Prof. Coulter a few days ago. He says he is to be in Washington for the next 6 months where he wishes to spend half of each day with me. I look forward to a most pleasant winter but how am I to do all my work!

He left our dear Walter Deane with mother Rose whom he loves so dearly. He would have nothing to do with either his mother or I when we returned.

I shall be in Washington about Sept. 1st. I fear it will be warm then but I must not be away any longer.

How you must be enjoying our summer. I long to spend a summer on the New England coast.

We have had such a restful time at Mother's Roses. The children are all so well and have grown so strong.

Walter Deane is such a good boy and how the other children do love him. I wish you could see him just as we do at home.

But I must close
Your friend
J. N. Rose

Washington D.C.
Dec 17/1897

My dear Deane:

I have been intending to answer your several good letters but from time to time my heart felt still I have had my hands pretty full. Joseph was taken with scarlet fever three weeks ago yesterday and the next day he was taken off to the hospital. It seemed like giving up our little boy for good, but he has without accident left hospital, and been so happy that we know now it was much the

[second page:]

You ask about Deana.
I shall publish a revision of the genus within the next week giving but 7 species. I have collected two of the species myself. I am publishing a synopsis of the Mexican Orchid life — In 1897 I collected 21 orchids. Such species belong to this order alone!

Dr Robinson has written protesting against Indiana name la mula. He finds it [illegible]

Seen nor [illegible] Jefferson's engagement and how it happened.
D[r?] Coulter is still here. He are [illegible] stupid on one hand [illegible] of the [illegible]

Yours truly
[signature]

better way to do. We were so anxious to keep the other children free from the dreadful disease. For the last three weeks we have been watching the other children very carefully for fear they would be taken sick. Rebecca started back to school on Tuesday. We hope to have Joseph home for Christmas. I ride out to see him every day after before breakfast.

We were dreadfully sorry you were not able to come on to see us. We have been

hoping that you would see our Walter Lorne while he is still a baby. He will soon be little man. He is a very jolly fellow and the pet of us all. I am sending you some pictures which I took just before leaving for Mexico last Spring but which were not finished until a few days ago. They are not very good but will show you that we really have such a boy as Walter Lorne even if you never have seen him.

My dear Deane: [Jan]
　　Your kind note of the 6th is just at hand. Yes our own boy is two years old, and what a fine strong boy he is. He can hardly believe that two years have passed since he came. You must not think of sending him any thing.
　　Little Martha has been very sick, but I am glad to write that she is better. I have just come from her window where I see her each day. Joseph is quite himself

again. If all goes well he and Rebecca will be in school again next Monday. The flu disease is nearly over. His cold and we hope he will miss the Scarlet fever. Miss Pine has had a very bad cold but is better now.

Our paper on Umbelliferae came out today. I think you will like what we have done with Donna. I will send you a copy as soon as I get my reprints.

Your friend

J M Rose

SMITHSONIAN INSTITUTION

UNITED STATES NATIONAL MUSEUM

S. P. LANGLEY
SECRETARY SMITHSONIAN INSTITUTION

WASHINGTON, D. C., Feb. 6, 1900.

Mr. Walter Deane,
    Cambridge Station, Boston, Mass.

My dear Deane:

    What material have you under Coelospermum gmelini from the eastern United States and are any of your specimens in fruit? This appears to be the Ligusticum actifolium of Michx. It may be that we will want to see your material but do not send it just now. If we need it I will send one of our boxes for it for it is really not safe to trust the herbarium specimens between ordinary binders boards.

        Yours very truly,

        C. More

        Assistant Curator,
            Division of Plants.

Washington D.C.
April 11th 1900

My dear Deane:

Your card at hand. Very glad to hear from you once more.

Yes you had better write to F. A. Lucas acknowledging the Seal books. It was through his kindness that the books were sent to you. I am pleased to learn that you obtained a set. The edition was small. I have not heard of the White Pine article but I will look it up soon.

Sorry to hear of the accident to p. Lairs...

Yes we are all well once more. Since I wrote you last however we have had more trouble. About three weeks after Martha came home Mrs. Rose was taken very sick and had to be sent to the hospital also

Here she had to undergo a rather serious operation. Although she was not gone long it seemed like weeks to us at home. She is quite her self again. Josepha and Martha are both as well as ever. It is interesting to hear them tell of their hospital experience.

Prof. Coulter and his family have gone back to Chicago. Our Revision is almost finished. It will contain numerous new species and several new genera. All the genera are to be illustrated.

I had a nice visit from Mr. Pringle last week.

Walter Deane is well. How he loves his fire engine and how he does make it fly across the room. We cannot get the little fellow to talk. He seems to understand everything we say but he will not try to use his tongue.

Mrs. Rose will add a line.

Your friend
J. N. Rose

Washington D.C.
April 17 1900.

My dear Deane!
　　　　Your two letters one to Mrs R & one to me — came yesterday and a great deal were we to hear from you. We were sorry to hear of your sister's sickness here in our city. I went around at once to enquire about her. I met your two nieces who are very delightful young ladies. Of course they had a great deal to say about you. They asked if you did not have some friends here and I said yes he knows all the botanists. Then one of them asked "But who has a little boy named for him." Mrs Rose wants your sister to see our

Walter Deane and as soon as she is better will take the little fellow down.

Lucas came to see me today, said he had heard from you and was delighted with your note. He said you certainly were one of the persons who should have a copy. Lucas is a good fellow and I am glad you wrote as you did.

You have named the little Umbel right only they call it now Levisticum. levisticum Koch. I suppose you know you had it in be Ligusticum in your published list. Can you give me the lady's name who sent you the fragment.

Love to all. hastily
J.N. Rose

Washington D.C.
June 24/1900

My dear Deane:

I was quite disgusted with myself when I looked at my watch Wednesday night and saw how very very late it was. I hope Mrs. D. will forgive me. Thursday morning I went down to Kneeland & Washington Sts. and bought 3 lbs. of the most freshest candy I have seen in a long time. I had it put up in three boxes. The candy had just been brought in and had not been taken out of the trays. The children were delighted with it and I want to thank you once more. Rebecca says she never did enjoy candy so much.

Then I went down to Frankies
- the same place you took me to -
were I bought some Haviland china
which seemed to please Mrs Roe
very much.
    I had a very pleasant trip down
the Sound. I remained over
in New York all day Friday taking
the Congressional in the evening for
Washington. Before leaving
New York I invested in a box
of 4th of July things.
    I found my family all well
and glad to see me.
    I had such a good time but
I owe much of it to you & Mrs
Deane.
    Mrs Roe joins in sending
love to Mrs Deane.
                Your friend
                    J. M. Roe

Washington D.C.
Sept. 16th 1900

My dear Deane:

I did not mean to let a whole Summer slip by without writing to you but the heat has been so great that we have done nothing outside of the ordinary duties of life. But we are thankful that we have all been well.

The children begin their school work tomorrow. It will be Martha's first day. How the little thing has looked forward to it. She is just so happy over it that she breaks out in a hearty laugh over the very thought of going to school.

I dont know how Master Walter Deane will get along without her for the two are so very devoted. Other children of course have close friendships but this one is a unique [?] one. He always speaks of her as "Dear". The other two children are always called by their own names but [Martin] is always "dear". He calls himself "Deane" and this has lead the other children to take up his name to some extent. Still we hope to have the whole name [taken?] up. I wish you could see him.

Our Umbelliferae paper is now all in galley and I hope a copy will be in your hands before another month.

I suppose Dr. Robinson will soon be home again. I am glad you have a copy of the Cyclopedia. Indeed it is a fine work. My second volume came a [little?] ago ago.

Dont wait for me to write and always call on me for help. I have not yet located those White pine papers. Our love to Mrs Deane.

Always J[?] Rose

My dear Deane:

I know it has been a long time since I heard from you but I had hoped to write before this. I have just had a long talk with Nelson about his visit at Cambridge and how much he enjoyed meeting you again. Your Cambridge people certainly did entertain your visitors in fine style.

Our Revision is still in press. I hope to see it out early next month. Did you ever get the pamphlet on the "White pine" and do you still want it?

We are all pretty well. Martha has had the Chicken pox, and Walter Deane is just taking them. He is feverish & cross. A year ago we were having scarlet fever.

I had a letter from Mr Pringle a few days ago saying that he was just leaving for home.

I trust you are all well. Give our love to Mrs Deane.

Nov. 29/1900

Your friend
JM

My dear Deane:

How good and thoughtful you are. And yet we have have let 2 weeks pass without saying a word. Every year since Joseph was a very little boy we have bought one or more of Ernest Nister's beautiful picture books. This year however we did not get one for some reason, but a very beautiful one did come from Boston. How these children all enjoy these pictures.

The lovely toy which came to little Walter Deane is a beauty. The whole family enjoyed it. I have just lifted the little man into his bed and find the key tied to his neck.

The children had a lovely Christmas and we enjoyed it seeing they were so happy.

I am glad you like the Monograph. It was a big piece of work and I am glad to have it behind me. I suppose you noticed it came out on the last day of the Century. I am now again at my Mexican work and have my other Contributions well along.

Dr Kennedy sent me a note acknowledging receipt of my last paper.

I wish you might see our big sturdy boy. I know you would say he was a fine fellow. We try to call him Willie Deane but he calls himself "Deane" and so the children also call him Deane. At first every one called him "Walter." He and Martha are very devoted to one another. They both wanted dolls for Christmas and so on Christmas morning when they saw their two dolls under the tree they threw

their arms about each other's neck and shouted with joy. How you would have enjoyed the sight. We have had three cases of Chickenpox but we are all quite well now.

Nelson left for Mexico last Sunday.

Miss Clark has been made Librarian in the Department of Agriculture.

I suppose you know that Tom Williams was dead. You know he was the lichen man.

We both send love to Mrs Deane

As ever
J M Coulter

Jan. 9/1901

Liberty Ind
Jan. 28/07

My dear Deane:
My brother died in Washington a week ago Sunday and I brought him home the next day. Poor Mother is broken hearted. Although he was 37 yet he was still her baby. I have not had the heart to go back to my own home. I must start back tomorrow.
Believe me Your friend

My dear Deane:

You kind letter of sympathy was received yesterday. Just how the sad accident occurred we shall never know. My brother had been with us for about a week expecting to leave on Monday. He had taken dinner with us on Saturday evening, leaving the house about 7 o'clock to spend the evening and night with a boy of his home town. He expected him back for a one o'clock dinner on Sunday but felt no uneasyness when he did not arrive on time. You can imagine what a shock it was to us to receive a telegram from Liberty asking if it was true that my brother was dead. He had then been dead

5 or 6 hours and had been taken to the undertaker. Just why the gas was turned on we cannot tell as both men were of course perfectly familiar with it. They had come in rather late but had deliberately gone to bed after carefully hanging up their clothes. Certain statements in the paper were not quite true. Poor Mother was heart broken. Her father too now 85 years old feels the loss most keenly and he depended so much on my brother. If there is any comfort in such occasions the sympathy of the home people furnished it. Hundreds of people called and the most beautiful flowers were sent from all parts of our state. The funeral was the largest held in the County during the last 20 years.

As the paper states, my brother was a farmer and owned a nice farm adjoining the town of Liberty. He lived with my grandfather and mother and looked after the formers farms as well as his own. His taking away seems like a dream.
My own family are well.
Your friend
J. J. Rose

Washington D.C.
Feb. 2 1907.

My dear Deane:

I hope you are planning to come down to Washington for a few days after your New York meeting. I know of several Washington people who will be very glad to see you.

Greenman came down and spent three or four hours with me last Tuesday. We had him out to dinner. Mrs Rine enjoyed meeting him very much.

We are all very well.

You will enjoy the envelope which I enclose.

Remember us all to Mrs Deane

In haste—

J.N.R.

Oct. 24/1907

My dear Deane:

Your good letter of the 9th is at hand. I am glad you liked the picture but I infer you did not quite understand it.

Joseph is not "holding on Walter Deane in his lap" but his brother George who is now 15 months old. The dear little baby is named for my brother. He is just now learning to walk. He is not so strong as Walter Deane but he has always been well. Walter Deane is a darling boy. The other morning he called to his mother to come and waken him. He and Martha continue the most devoted of friends. They are both full of Christmas.

Yes I have seen Bailey's new paper. How he does turn off the work. I suppose you know that Scribner is to leave Washington.

I suppose Mr. Greenman is again back in Cambridge. I wish I could get him on here for awhile.

We all hope you and Mrs. Deane can come on next fall to the A.O.U.

I would like to get up to Cambridge in the Spring but don't see my way clear just now. I wish you might see my Mexican blankets and I am sure Mrs. Deane would enjoy Mrs. Rice's Mexican drawn work.

I hope to get Mr. Greenman on for a few months this winter.

Mr. Pollard hopes to go to Cuba in a few weeks.

I suppose Sargent's new work will be something fine. He has just written to me asking for my help.

Give our love to Mrs. Deane. My wife is busy dressing dolls tonight. Dec 20/97 Your friend
JaRoe

My dear Dearie:

For more than a week I have tried to write to you and thank you for your Christmas greetings which you sent to all the Roses. How we did enjoy opening the package! The children usually get so many things Christmas morning that we thought best to look into your package Christmas Eve. How kind of you to send another of those beautiful Miller picture books. They contain the most beautiful pictures for children that are published. How Walter Deane does love the book. He really goes to bed with it. The Audubon Calendar is very choice and Mrs. Rose too both wish to thank you for it.

We had a very nice Christmas for

the day was given up to the little ones. We had the tree as usual. This is really Walter Dean's first Christmas for last year he was too young to enjoy it.

We also received the card for baby George. He is such a dear little fellow. I ought to have told you about the little fellow along time ago but I hoped you would come down and we would have a little surprise for you.

We are all quite well.

Your friend,

J M Roe

Washington D.C.
Jan 12th 1902

My dear Mr. Deane:

How very good of you to remember our little boy so very generously on his birthday. How very happy the little fellow was and how he still treasures every bit of packing about the bright coin. When Rebecca came home from school, the day his present came, he announced to her that "Mr. Deane had sent him a penny and two cottons." He still keeps the "cottons" but the gold has gone to the bank to start his account as you suggest. I have obtained one of those little savings banks so new to Washington but old in other cities. You have doubtless seen them.

They are called branch banks while the children keep in their homes but the banker keeps the key.

We had a lovely day with a cake & candles at night. I know you would enjoy your namesake if you could see him. He is everything, and more, that you describe except mischievous. He is just the dearest boy and the pet of us all. You must see him before an other year.

We all send love to both you & Mrs Deane.

Your friend,
J. Mose

SMITHSONIAN INSTITUTION

UNITED STATES NATIONAL MUSEUM

S. P. LANGLEY
  Secretary, Smithsonian Institution
RICHARD RATHBUN
  Assistant Secretary, in charge of
    U. S. National Museum

WASHINGTON, D. C., April 20, 1905.

Mr. Walter Deane,

    Cambridge, Mass.

My dear Mr. Deane:-

    I am sending you a specimen, a rather poor one I know, but you will doubtless be glad to have it in your collection. It is a new species of **Deanea** which I have just described but not yet published. I have also just written up a description of <u>D.pringlei</u>, sent out by Mr. Pringle in 1901 under no. 8601. We have just sent you volume 9, of the Contributions from the U. S. National Herbarium, Plants of Guam, and volume 8, no.4, containing a little paper of mine, will be sent you in a day or two. I hope you will be pleased with these papers.

    Yours very truly,

    J.N.Rose

    Associate Curator,

        Division of Plants.

LIBERTY HERALD.

Jan 24, PHONE 32, 1901

C. H. & I. TIME TABLE.

TRAINS PASS LIBERTY AS FOLLOWS:

EAST BOUND
- No. 85 Express, Daily............ 8:53 A.M.
- No. 21 Fast Mail, Daily........... 10:45 A.M.
- No. 37 Accom, Daily except Sunday 12:31 P.M.
- No. 41 Exp., Daily except Sunday... 4:31 P.M.
- No. 83 Express, Daily (Don't stop) 6:37 P.M.
- No. 89 Accom, Daily.............. 9:30 P.M.

WEST BOUND
- No. 84 Fast Mail, Daily........... 4:76 A.M.
- No. 40 Accom, Daily............... 9:35 A.M.
- No. 85 Express, Daily............. 1:34 P.M.
- No. 88 Accom, Daily except Sunday 4:43 P.M.
- No. 84 Express, Daily............. 7:06 P.M.
- No. 86 Express, Daily............. 10:53 P.M.
(Stops on Flag Sundays)
(Stops only Ing. 84)

IN MEMORIAM.

GEORGE W. ROSE.

George W. Rose was born Aug. 29, 1863 on a farm near Liberty, Ind. His father, George Rose, was a soldier in war, a member of the 9th Ind. Calvary. He was taken sick a few days before he intended starting home, at Vicksburg, and died there in a hospital, a soldier's death, Aug. 9th, 1863. Since the death of his father George and his mother have lived together with his grandfather Mr. Joseph Corrington. George had an only brother, Dr. J. N. Rose, of Washington D. C., who is here today.

It needs no long memorial from me today. The people of this town, community and county loved him and know his character. The people would pay a tribute to the one they loved and honored, and as one of the people, as their representative I will, in my humble way, endeavor to speak at this time. The people are even no more to-day, mourning for their friend with a sorrow too deep for tears, and too wide to compass with words. The friends at large who lovers of their friend, in the presence of two great mysteries, life and death, with sorrowing hearts meet, to-day at the side of this still, unconscious house of clay to speak a few words of kindness, of regret, of love and hope.

Little need be said of the life George Rose lived among the people. He won and held a place of honor and esteem in the hearts of all who knew him. He met the aggravations of life with a smile and greeted all with a laugh and cheery word, leaving behind him a sweet, sustaining influence that pours its tide into the depths of eternity. Such an influence goes forth to the world as silently as the morning light, as strong as human affection. It would not be saying too much to say that fewer men had more friends than George Rose. He won them to him by his gentle, masterful, unassuming way. His actions, true and steadfast...

brother and affectionate kindred could teach and throw around him. The kindness in him shone from his eyes and reflected from his countenance. Thus he met the world; thus he went its friendly cheer; thus he kept the multitude nigh unto him in bonds of love and fidelity.

Two weeks ago, looking into day, he bid the people good bye, he set on a journey full of hopeful happiness. His generous heart throbbed with joyful anticipation. The good byes to us were like a summer breeze; now turned into a torrent of woe. He went from us as the brooks sing that wind and babble through the fields where his herds wander and feed and his plow turns the early springtime furrow. Went from us as they run on in glee and gladness, laughing on their way to the sea.

Particulars of the sad ending you will learn from your county papers. On the home coming we will not dwell. It is too heavy with grief for words to lighten. There is but one power alone that can lift it; can lighten the darkness and gloom and send peace unto our souls. That power must come from our divine Master, he who guides a flock of clustering stars across the pathway of night and holds as toys in His hands the mountains of the valleys, whose granite peaks rend the folds of summer and winter clouds as they pass by.

God takes care of His trusting ones, who hold on to His extended hand as the surges rise, and the heavens are wild with meeting clouds. It is then He often whispers peace, and the gloom is broken by a gushing radiance from the rifted folds of the tempest, and the melody of a purer sphere fills the sky arching lovingly life's slumbering sea. Sadly and mournfully we say farewell until the Master bids us come and then we'll understand.

This was the man we loved—are loving yet,
And still shall love, while longing eyes are wet
With selfish tears that well were brushed away,
Remembering his smile of yesterday.

For, even as we knew him, smiling still, Somewhere, beyond all earthly ache or ill He waits, with the old welcome—just as when
We met him smiling; we shall meet again.

W. H.

ALBERT E. MILLER.

Albert Edward Miller was born at Liberty, Indiana, Sept. 22nd, 1870. This son, who came to the home of Theodore Miller, and Anna Templeton Miller, was a beautiful child, of precious brightness, with a sunny, lovable nature, that won the hearts of all, and brought much sweetness and light into the lives of many. As a child he had exceptional confidence in his parents, yielding a cheerful obedience, and so, under the watchful care of an in...

...last summer, the deceased, with means provided by himself, visited Paris and other cities in Europe. Returning in the fall, he renewed his employment in Washington, where he had already won many true friends. At last's employer, Mr. T. B. Marshall, in letter...

...found your son from after a despair to, a few hours ago, loved by everyone. Unexpectedly, and mercifully painless, death came in the morning hours of Sunday, Jan. 20th, closing this sunny and happy life at the early age of twenty-one years. "The leaf has perished in the green," leaving undeveloped possibilities. But those who knew him most intimately, believing that his affection and gratitude would never have failed in any great demand, cannot doubt that this life, ripened in maturer years, would have been as a staff to the father and mother, when their declining days came, and, rich in kindly and generous acts, yielded much helpfulness and happiness to a wide circle of friends.

M. H.

burg, and died there in a hospital, a soldiers death, Aug. 9th, 1863. Since the death of his father George and his mother have lived together with his grand-father Mr. Joseph Corrington. George had an only brother, Dr. J. N. Rose, of Washington D. C., who is here today.

It needs no long memorial from me today. The people of this town, community and county loved him and know his character. The people would pay a tribute to the one they loved and honored, and as one of the people, as their representative I will, in my humble way, endeavor to speak at this time. The people are to-day mourners to-day, mourning for their friend with a sorrow too deep for tears, and too wide to compass with words. The friends at large who lovers of their friend, in the presence of two great mysteries, life and death, with sorrowing hearts meet to-day at the side of this still, unconscious house of clay to speak a few words of kindness, of regret, of love and hope.

Little need be said of the life George Rose lived among the people. He won and held a place of honor and esteem in the hearts of all who knew him. He met the aggravations of life with a smile and greeted all with a laugh and cheery word, leaving behind him a sweet, sustaining influence that pours its tide into the depths of eternity. Such an influence goes forth to the world as silently as the morning light; as strong as human affection. It would not be saying too much to say that fewer men had more friends than George Rose. He won them to him by his gentle, masterful, unassuming way. His actions, true and steadfast, held the friendship given. Actions speak more eloquently and loudly in men's every day life than the roll of gathered thunders, or the roar of ocean rising in wrath at the whisper of its king. All men were his brethren. His vocation in life by choice, was that of a farmer. In this he was prosperous. He was frugal in his wants and desires, and satisfied to live and work among the fields where the birds whistled their wild notes of gladness, and health and abundance came from the breast of the soil. Public notice he sought not after, and he cared naught for public office and its emoluments. Raised and nurtured under the best and sweetest of home influences, he learned lessons of purity, devotion of purpose and nobleness of character, he grew up blest with health and a cheerful mind. He was fond of his home. Leaving for a time, he always returned to it like a bird to its nest, blithe and happy. The precepts taught George Rose, in this, his dear home, were the loftiest, and best that a loving grand-father, a doting mother, a devoted

a flock of clustering stars across the pathway of night and holds as toys in His hands the mountains of the valleys, whose granite peaks, rend the folds of summer and winter clouds as they pass by.

God takes care of his trusting ones, who hold on to His extended hand as the surges rise, and the heavens are wild with meeting clouds. It is then He often whispers peace, and the gloom is broken by a gushing radiance from the rifted folds of the tempest, and the melody of a purer sphere fills the sky arching lovingly life's slumbering son. Sadly and mournfully we say farewell until the Master bids us come, and then we'll understand.

This was the man we loved—are loving yet
And still shall love, while longing eyes are wet
With selfish tears that well were brushed away,
Remembering his smile of yesterday.
For, even as we knew him, smiling still,
Somewhere, beyond all earthly ache or ill
He waits, with the old welcome—just as when
We met him smiling; we shall meet again.

.W. H.

ALBERT E. MILLER.

Albert Edward Miller was born at Liberty, Indiana, Sept. 22nd, 1879. This son, who came to the home of Theodore Miller, and Anna Templeton Miller, was a beautiful child, of precious brightness, with a sunny, lovable nature, that won the hearts of all, and brought much sweetness and light into the lives of many. As a child he had exceptional confidence in his parents, yielding a cheerful obedience, and so, under the watchful care of an indulgent and affectionate father and mother, and in the loving and perfect companionship of an older sister, a happy childhood was passed.

As he grew through boyhood years to young manhood, his sunny temperament predominated, although other qualities of disposition disclosed themselves—affection and generosity in abundant measure—a youth of many noble traits. His buoyancy of spirit attracted. Friendship and affection came to him unsought.

Through desire, not of necessity, he left his home at the early age of eighteen years, to enter, in a city, the struggle for a livelihood. It cannot be, expected otherwise than that this is followed by hardships, and the courageous way in which one so young took upon himself the problem of self-support, was evidence of great self-reliance.

During the years of his absence from home his parents received regularly from him cheerful letters, and other evidences that his affectionate regard for them had not lessened.

The last two years of this short life were passed largely in Washington, D.

Friends Die Together

Boyhood Companions the Victims of Illuminating Gas.

George W. Rose and Albert E. Miller Asphyxiated in the Latter's Room.

The Washington Times of Monday contains the following particulars of the death of George Rose and Albert Miller:

Locked in each others arms, George W. Rose and Albert Miller, who had passed their boyhood together in Liberty, Ind., were found dead in bed in a second story back room in the boarding house of Mrs. Elizabeth Faunce, 636 Fifth Street, northwest, about 11:30 o'clock yesterday morning. The room was filled with gas, and every indication pointed to their deaths having been caused by accidental asphyxiation. Miller had been rooming in the house for about a month, and was generally looked upon as steady and reliable.

Saturday night Mrs. Faunce lighted a gas stove in his room to have the apartment warm when he should return, but as he was not in bed by 1:30 o'clock in the morning, she concluded that he would remain out all night, and cutting off the supply of gas, allowed the stove to cool. She had hardly returned to her room when she heard Miller enter the house and go direct to his room. He was conversing with some one at the time, and she concluded that he had brought some one home with him. She thought nothing further regarding the matter until shortly after 11 o'clock yesterday morning, when she detected a strong odor of gas in the upper part of the house, and traced it to the room occupied by Miller.

Mrs. Faunce became alarmed, and endeavored to enter the room, but the door was locked, and she had to call a colored boy, who is employed in the house, to assist her in forcing an entrance into the room. After the door was opened it was several minutes before the room was sufficiently cleared of the escaping gas to permit of her entering. When she did so she saw at a glance that the two men were beyond all human aid. They were lying on the bed locked in each other's arms. She immediately notified the police, and Policeman Coghill was sent from the Sixth precinct station-house to make an investigation, and take charge of the bodies until the arrival of Coroner Nevitt, who in the meantime had been notified.

Mrs. Faunce told the Coroner that she found the gas jet in the room turned about half on, while a full head of gas was escaping from the stove.

From Mrs. Faunce it was learned that Miller was employed at the Lockmann Cafe, and Thomas R. Marshall, the proprietor, was communicated with. After Coroner Nevitt had issued a certificate of accidental death, Mr. Marshall directed that the remains of both men should be taken charge of and removed to the undertaking establishment of Joseph Gawler, 1734 Pennsylvania Avenue northwest, until their relatives should be heard from. He also telegraphed to Theodore Miller, the father of his former employee, at Liberty, Ind.

Meanwhile Dr. Joseph N. Rose, who is the assistant botanist at the National Museum, was waiting patiently at his home, 1001 Third Street, LeDroit Park, for the return of his brother, who the evening before had told him that he had met an old friend and would probably spend the night with him, but that he would be back to his brother's house early Sunday morning. Nothing was heard from him all day long and it was not until about dusk that he was surprised by the receipt of a telegram from his mother Mrs. Rebecca Rose, at Liberty, stating that a message had been received there that George had been asphyxiated and that she wished to know if it was true.

When Dr. Rose called at Gawler's undertaking rooms he identified his brother's body and stated that he had been visiting him at his home and that he arrived in the city about a week ago. His brother George he said, was a well-to-do farmer, who had never married, thirty-eight years old, and that he had started out on his present trip in search of both pleasure and recreation. He had planned to leave Washington this evening for Old Point Comfort and from there he intended to continue his trip to Savannah and probably to some Florida point. His clothing, which was of the finest texture, gave evidence to his being a man of means, while the other possessions which were found in his clothes showed him to be an educated man of taste. He had a handsome gold watch and chain, with a charm set in diamonds, a magnificent solitaire diamond ring, and a pocketbook containing a $20 bill and a draft drawn on the Western National Bank of New York for $108 by the Citizens' Bank of Liberty, Ind. and payable to George W. Rose. The draft was signed by William F. Kennedy as cashier of the Liberty bank, but had not been endorsed by the payee. It was dated January 10, 1901 and was numbered 2295. There were also two blank checks in the pocket book on the same bank.

Miller, who was a single man, has been employed at the Lockmann as a waiter for nearly two years. Last summer during the dull season he took a trip to Europe and visited the fair in Paris. He was always looked upon as a steady and reliable man, and one who knew how to save his money. At the time of his death he had about $50 in the care of Mr. Marshall, and in his room was $11.50 in small change. His father is a clerk in a dry goods store in Liberty. His only sister married Albert Thompson, a prominent business man of Indianapolis, where she is said to be a social leader.

The bodies of the young men, accompanied by Dr. J. N. Rose, arrived in Liberty Tuesday morning at 10 o'clock. The funeral services of Albert Miller were conducted at the home of his parents, Mr. and Mrs. Theodore Miller, Wednesday morning at 10 o'clock by Rev. D. W. Parks. The funeral of George Rose took place Wednesday afternoon at the home of Joseph Corrington conducted by Rev. D. W. Parks.

LIBERTY HERALD.
PHONE 32
OFFICIAL PAPER OF UNION COUNTY.

C. W. STIVERS & SONS,
Editors, Publishers and Proprietors.

LIBERTY, INDIANA.
THURSDAY, January 24, 1901.

My dear Deane:

It was so good of you and Mrs Deane to call so soon on Mrs Stuart. I am sorry you missed her both times. Both Mrs Roe and I wished you to meet Mrs Stuart, for we all think so much of her. We have not heard from her since she left New York. I hope she took your address to her fine machine. She spent three weeks here with Mrs Roe before going North. You don't know how glad I was to get home although

I did have a very good time. I met so many people I had been writing to for years but had never seen like Mrs Parish, Dr Shreve, Prof. Nolan, Prof. Lombard etc. It was interesting to hear Mrs Parish tell of Dr Gray's visit to Ami many years ago.

I was three weeks at Tucson the guest of the Desert Laboratory of the Carnegie Institution. I had a cottage all to myself. The brown mountains all about the valley were very interesting. I was collecting Cacti chiefly and what a quantity I did get!

Berry thinks Hadley Bluff here (pinkroot). Vernonia many in bloom have, some of the field. How I'm [missing?] the poor Manual he [ed?] out?

We are all very well. The children are all out of bed. Rebecca has gone to Hartford for a week. However we all send much love.

Sincerely
J Apger

June 28/1928

My dear Dare:

It has been a long long time since I have written you but I have often thought of you and we often talk of you. We want to go to Boston next year and will then see you if not before. Mrs [?] had such a good time at Baltimore and now wants to go the Boston meeting of the A.A.S.
Dr J M Coalter & family will arrive in Washington

I do not know when I can another trip although I would like to get away this spring. I am just now busy with all kinds of proof reading and will soon have some more papers to send you.
I trust you and Mrs Dare are both well. We all send love.

Your friend
[signature]

Jan 10/1909

Tuesday morning for a week stay. They are on their way to Europe for a year. Saturday night we give a party for them. Wish you could be here.

Thank you very much for remembering us all on Christmas. Lewis's Revel is a fine story and we have all enjoyed it very much. Walter Deane liked the book you sent him. He thinks there is no one like you. I wish you could see him again before he is gone.

He was delighted with his birthday present. He always's faithful Michael presents his little saving bank. Mrs. Rae is expecting her cousin Mrs. Stuart next week. He is still busy. Very excited to Thanksgiving. What is this Rowdies this winter? Is it coming soon? We are all very well. The children had a lovely Christmas.

CHAIRMAN
GEORGE M. KOBER
1819 Q Street, N. W.

SECRETARY
JAMES H. GORE
2110 R Street, N. W.

BUILDING COMMITTEE
Washington Academy of Sciences
CO-OPERATING WITH
The George Washington Memorial Association

WASHINGTON, D. C. June 13/09

JOB BARNARD
MARCUS BENJAMIN
THOMAS BLAGDEN
H. F. BLOUNT
W. B. BRYAN
D. S. CARL
A. P. DAVIS
J. S. DILLER
B. W. EVERMANN
JOHN W. FOSTER
G. H. GROSVENOR
ARNOLD HAGUE
WALTER HOUGH
RUDOLPH KAUFFMANN
G. W. LITTLEHALES
T. N. McLAUGHLIN
C. HART MERRIAM
WILLIS MOORE
J. D. PATTEN
GIFFORD PINCHOT
G. R. PUTNAM
E. B. ROSA
J. N. ROSE
W. H. SEAMAN
CH. WARDELL STILES
J. S. STONE
H. W. WILEY

My dear Deane:

It has been a long long time since I heard from you and a still longer time since I have written myself. Still I often hear about you through your friends; Brewster Collins and others. Just now I have one of your local botanists for an assistant, Moore.

I have had a very busy winter and I think much has been accomplished. P. N. Coulter has been here until 10 days ago occupying a table in my office. I was in New York City last week finishing up a Revision of Cereus — which Dr Britton and I will soon publish.

We are now all pretty well. Mrs. Rose spent two weeks in a hospital and while she was away George was very sick at home. Joe has just gone to New Mexico where he is to spend the summer with the Geological Survey. Rebecca has remained at home with her mother all winter. We hope to send her to college next winter.

Walter Deane grows and grows. He is a fine boy. I wish you might see him before he is a man. He enjoys your letters and often talks about you. He declares that he will go to Harvard College.

Mrs Rose and I often talk about you and wish we might see you again. Give our heart love to Mrs Deane and believe me your friend

J. W. Rose

SMITHSONIAN INSTITUTION
UNITED STATES NATIONAL MUSEUM
WASHINGTON, D. C.

February 16, 1911.

Mr. Walter Deane,
   29 Brewster Place,
      Cambridge, Mass.

My dear Deane:

      Please pardon me for not answering sooner your letter of January 23d, with letter of Elmer Stearns. This is the fourth letter of Stearns that has come to me within the last few weeks, one from Mr. Coville, one from Dr. Britton and one to me personally, but this is by far the best. It is good enough to read before your Botanical Club. I know Stearns, having met him several times on my various field trips. He is a good fellow, but does not know very much botany. He shows his weak points strongest in his letters. After you have read one of them you can then understand why it is that he is a Christian Scientist.

      You will be surprised to learn that I am leaving for Mexico again. This week, I start for Lower California. At San Diego I take the Government vessel "Albatross" to sail around Lower California, making numerous stops for the purpose of collecting cacti.

                                      Yours very truly,

                                      J M Rose

                              Associate Curator, Div. of Plants.

RL

(Enclosure.)

Carnegie Institution of Washington
DEPARTMENT OF BOTANICAL RESEARCH

Smithsonian Institution, Washington, D. C.,
February 6, 1912.

Mr. Walter Deane,
   29 Brewster Street,
      Cambridge, Massachusetts.

My dear Mr. Deane:

      You will be interested to learn, I am quite sure, that I have asked for a furlough from the National Museum and have been transferred to the Carnegie Institution, and have already begun my work of preparing an exhaustive monograph on the Cactaceae of North and South America. It is with considerable regret that I sever my relations with the National Museum, with which I have been connected for so long; but the offer of the Carnegie Institution opens up so many possibilities that I could not very well decline it. The enclosed letter will show you the scope of my work.

    As you are aware, only one cactus is to be found in all New England. Would it be too much trouble for you to give me the records, so far as you know, for Opuntia in New England, and what localities for the plant in Eastern United States are shown by your herbarium specimens?

                      Yours very truly,

                              Research Associate.

CARNEGIE INSTITUTION OF WASHINGTON

Washington, D. C.

Office of the President   January 31st, 1912.

Dr. J. N. Rose,
    U. S. National Museum,
        Washington, D. C.

Dear Dr. Rose:

        I am pleased to inform you that at a meeting of our Executive Committee held on the 18th instant, you were appointed a Research Associate of the Department of Botanical Research of the Institution for the year 1912, and that an allotment for your personal compensation at the rate of $300 per month was made.

        The object of this association is, as has already been explained to you by Dr. MacDougal, to secure your cooperation and that of Dr. N. L. Britton, of the New York Botanical Garden, along with that of our Department of Botanical Research, in the prosecution of a general investigation of the cactus family of plants.

        Under the supervision of Dr. MacDougal, Director of the Department of Botanical Research, there will be available also for this special work the following allotments, namely:

```
          Salary of an assistant..................$1,500.
          Exploration and travel..................  1,400.
          Expenses of an artist for 5 months......    500.
                                                  $3,400.
```

        I would suggest that you take up correspondence concerning this matter immediately with Dr. Cannon, who is the Acting Director of the Department in the absence of Dr. MacDougal.

In the meantime, if you will let me know when you will be ready to have your compensation begin, I shall be glad to instruct our Bursar to make payments in accordance with your wishes, both on account of your own compensation and that of your assistant. Since I understand that you have already been engaged to some extent in this work, if the Secretary of the Smithsonian Institution approves, your compensation may date from the beginning of the current year if desirable. I leave this matter for your decision, however.

Permit me to assure you of a warm personal interest in the research you and your colleagues are to undertake and of a desire to give you all assistance practicable from the Institution's office of administration. I have long known Dr. Britton, and I am sure that he, Dr. MacDougal and yourself will make one of the strongest teams available for such a fine field of work.

                Very truly yours,

                    (Signed) R. S. Woodward.

My dear Deane:

How we have all enjoyed your letters and your Christmas gifts this year! Your book was such a good one. Mr. Pier read it one night until midnight and another night until 1:15. How we did enjoy it! Walter Deane will be 15 tomorrow. Can you believe it? The little boy you once saw and the one I once wrote you about is little no more.

He is now nearly six feet tall, taller than his father. I wish you might see him in his cadet uniform. He is a fine looking fellow. He wants to go to Harvard and I think we must send him there. He is doing well in school especially in Latin. Do you think it would be well to send to him to some preparatory school which will fit him for Harvard?

Mrs. Rowe and I often told of you and Mrs. Deane. I know Mrs. Deane must have her hand quite full. My mother is situated much in the same way. Her father with whom she live & care for will be 97 this month.

I leave for the West Indies on January 24th. I expect to visit all the West Indian islands so far as possible. I shall be away about 10 weeks. We are all quite well. We all send you love

Your friend
M.

Jan 5 1912

The Tribune Tavern
W. A. BROUSE, PROPR.
TRIBUNE : KANSAS

My dear Deane:—
 I left Mrs. Rose and the children at Lafayette, Ind. last Monday and came out here to Western Kansas to look for Cacti.
 I trust you & Mrs. Deane are both quite well.
  Yours very truly
  J. Rose

Sept. 17/ 1912

SMITHSONIAN INSTITUTION
UNITED STATES NATIONAL MUSEUM
WASHINGTON, D. C.

October /2, 1912.

Mr. Walter Deane,
    29 Brewster Street,
        Cambridge, Massachusetts.

My dear Deane:

        I have been intending ever since my return to write to you regarding the bridges of Paris. Your two letters were duly received while I was in Europe and when in Paris I made repeated efforts to obtain pictures of the bridges you wanted, but unfortunately I was not able to find any of them. I did pick up, however, a few photographs of some other bridges, and these I am sending to you. I have a few pictures of bridges in Rome and some other European cities which I shall be glad to send to you if you would care to have them.

        Yours very truly,

The Pont-Neuf.- *   *   * In the 17th and 18th cent. the Pont-Neuf was the favorite rendez-vous of news vendors, jugglers, showmen, loungers, and thieves. To this motley crowd Tabarin, a famous satirist, used to spout his witticisms, from a platform which he set up between Nos. 13 and 15 in the Place du Pont-Neuf. One of the first hydraulic pumps, the 'Samaritaine', was erected on this bridge (model at the Musée Carnavalet). Near by are the swimming-baths of 'La Samaritaine'. Down below, behind the statue of the king, is the Jardin Henri IV or Jardin du Vert-Galant. The best view of the bridge is obtained from this garden or from the banks of the Seine. Secondhand book stalls line the quays.

Opposite the equestrian statue, a few paces distant, is the Place Dauphine (Called Place de Thionville under the Revolution), partly surrounding which are some 17th cent. houses of brick, with festoons of white stone.

The Pont de la Concorde (Pl. R, 15, 14; II), which crosses the Seine from the Place de La Concorde to the Chambre des Deputes was built by Perronet in 1787-90, the material for the upper part being furnished by the stones of the Bastille. The piers are in the form of half-columns, and were adorned with statues (now at Versailles).

The view from the bridge is very fine. It includes the Place de la Concorde, the Madeleine, and the Chamber of Deputies; then, upstream, to the left, the Tuileries Garden, a pavilion of the Tuileries and one of the Louvre, the Pont Solferino and the Pont-Royal; to the right, the Gare du Qaui-d'Orsay, in front of which is the little dome of the Palais de la Legion d'Honneur; farther off are the dome of the Institut, the towers of Notre Dame, the spire of the Sainte-Chapelle, and the dome of the Tribunal de Commerce. Downstream, to the right, appear the Palais in the Champs-Elysees; then the Pont Alexandre Trois, and the towers of the Trocadero; to the left the Ministry of Foreign Affairs and the inevitable Eiffel Tower. The dome of the Invalides can be seen only from a little below the bridge, to the right of the Chamber of Deputies.

My dear Mr. Deane:
Your kind letter is at hand. Please express to Mrs. Deane our sympathy. Mrs. Rce would have written at once but she has been sick in bed for two days. We have often had you both in mind during the winter knowing how full your hands & hearts must be.

We have made no definite plans for the Summer.

mother "Cactaceae Epiphyllum and its allies." This cactus work of mine is very interesting but it is a bigger task than I thought.

Write to us when you can and tell how you are getting along.

Your friend
J. N. Rose
June 12/913

I had thought some of spending a month or so at Cambridge and working at the Gray Herbarium but to bring my whole family would make it very expensive. We are hoping now to locate near New York City. This will make it easy for me to spend much time at the New York Botanical Garden.

Martha graduates next Monday at High School. Can you believe it?

I have just sent you

Carnegie Institution of Washington
DEPARTMENT OF BOTANICAL RESEARCH

Smithsonian Institution, Washington, D. C.,
January 20, 1913.

Mr. Walter Deane,
    29 Brewster Street,
        Cambridge, Massachusetts.

My dear Deane:

    Yesterday I took out a package of bridges, mostly from Italy and Switzerland, which I thought you might be glad to have for your collection. These go off to-day. In the meantime, your very kind letter was received this morning, and has been read with a great deal of interest.

    I leave for St. Thomas next Saturday morning. My address during February and the greater part of March will be: "Care, Emile A. Berne, Agent, Quebec Steamship Company, Charlotte Amelie, St. Thomas, West Indies." It is our intention to visit Porto Rico, many of the Lesser Antilles, Curacao, and possibly the northern coast of South America. I hardly expect to reach Trinidad; but in case I do, I shall certainly call on your friends there.

                      Yours very truly,

                              Research Associate.

My dear Deane:

have been intend-
ing for some time to write
to you [illegible] you kind
loan of to [illegible] of
this [illegible] not fly. was
so glad to hear from you
while [illegible] was in [illegible]
[illegible] India. [illegible]
interesting [illegible] [illegible] [illegible]
could not cover as [illegible]
[illegible] as [illegible] had [illegible]
then, I have brought it
back [illegible] [illegible] correction

We have just been looking
over **Worcester** [illegible] my
what do you think of
it? [illegible]
[illegible] Hopkinson [illegible] [illegible]
[illegible] I think?
We have [illegible] [illegible] of Domsly
at Cambridge England [illegible]
[illegible]
[illegible]
[illegible]
[illegible]
May 8 14

of all kind of plants etc
especially Cacti.

My Cactus which does grow
+ only one, an it will
take [?] to do it
right.

I [?] we
shall do this Summer.
would like to [?]
of the city of Cambridge
where I would spend
some time, [?] each
week in a large
herbarium. You [?]

don't know if any one
[?] Cambridge who will
[?] have [?]
take their house for
about 2 months?

[?] is just [?]
ing his first year
in High School. [?]
I will keep him here
one other year. I [?]
sometimes if you [?] it
it would be best to put
him into a [?] preparatory
school, or [?]. [?]
do you think about it?

Liberty Ind –

My dear Deane:

While in New York at work last week I received word that my mother's father had died and I came on at once. He was nearly 98 years old! I have had my home with him ever since my father's death in 1864. I was named for him. I hope to get back to my family and work next

I suppose you saw the notice in the Outlook. When I get home I will write you a long letter. My love to Mrs Deane.

Your friend

J. P. Rice

Aug. 1/1913

week but mother will need me a few days longer.

It has been 10 days since I saw my family!

Walter Deane is at work on the Robert E. Lee farm near Washington which is used by the Department of Agriculture.

I have been intending to write ever since Mrs. Deane's father died. What a fine man he was.

WESTERN UNION
TELEGRAM
THEO. N. VAIL, PRESIDENT

Form 1864

RECEIVED AT
3ONYMB 10

15 Boylston St., Harvard Sq.,
Cambridge, Mass.

WASHINGTON DC MAR 2-3-1914-

MR WALTER DEANE,

29 BREWSTER ST CAMBRIDGE MASS

WALTER DEANE WAS KILLED IN A STREET CAR ACCIDENT TODAY

J N ROSE   103 P MAR 3 1914

STAR, WEDNESDAY, MARCH 4, 1914.

CADETS TO ATTEND FUNERAL

Tribute by Western High School Companies to Deceased Comrade.

Both companies of cadets from the Western High School are to attend, as organizations and in uniform, the funeral of Walter D. Rose, a pupil at that institution, and a member of Company H of the Cadet Regiment, who was knocked from a street car and killed Monday near 34th and O streets. The services will be held at the Church of the Covenant, Connecticut avenue and N street northwest, with Rev. Charles Wood, pastor of the church, officiating.

Dr. Wood will be assisted by Rev. Mr. Hannaford, assistant pastor of the church, and by Rev. Bernard Braskamp, until recently assistant minister and now pastor of Gurley Memorial Church. Interment will be in Rock Creek cemetery.

Young Rose was a member of the Church of the Covenant, where he served as an usher and was one of the active young men in the Sunday school.

Sunday, March 15/1914.

My dear Deane:

You must pardon my not writing sooner to you but I could not write before, and yet you have been constantly in my thoughts. Not only did our dear boy bear your name but you have been in all our thoughts & plans for him. I remember that you were the first of our friends who we told of his birth. Then he was

You don't know how much we wanted you to see and know our dear boy and now he has been taken away from us! We are trying to be brave but this is so hard to give him up. Both you and Mrs Deane have been so good to write. I will try and write again soon.

We all send dearest love — your friend
M Drew

not baptized as a babe like the others but we said we will wait until Mr. & Mrs. Deane come. Year after we planned to have you both to come & we talked again & again about going to you but there were several long lean years and these were followed by the war and we could not go. My promotions came at regular intervals but with them came added burdens. But we constantly talked about you & planned for meetings which never came. I wrote you I know how the little boy was growing & at last that he was a young man & that next year he would go to school & be near you. He wanted to go to Boston at Christmas time and worked hard all summer with this constantly in view. Then he planned to come this Spring or we talked about having you & Mrs Deane to come here.

You don't know how much we wanted you to see and know our dear boy and now he has been taken away from us! We are trying to be brave but this so hard to give him up. Both you and Mrs Deeme have been so good to write. I will try and write again soon.

We all send dearest love. Your friend
Mori

My dear Deane;

Thank you very very much for your good letter. We are all pretty well except Mrs. Rice. She is just heartbroken over the death of our dear boy. She was so proud of him & loved him so.

We were out to his grave on Monday and found the flowers almost as beautiful as when we left them 10 days before. The snow seemed to have kept them just at the right temperature.

I am sending you the report made by the Principal of the Salem High School. Will you please return it to me.

Martha has returned to Oxford Ohio & Joseph to Liberty.

Give our love to Mrs Deane

Your friend,
J. H. Rice

March 20 / 1914

CARNEGIE INSTITUTION OF WASHINGTON
DEPARTMENT OF BOTANICAL RESEARCH

COASTAL LABORATORY, CARMEL, CALIFORNIA   DESERT LABORATORY, TUCSON, ARIZONA

Smithsonian Institution, Washington, D. C.,

April 14, 1914.

Mr. Walter Deane,
   29 Brewster Street,
      Cambridge, Massachusetts.

My dear Mr. Deane:

      I have been intending to write you for some time to answer some of the questions you asked me regarding the street car accident. The car on which the accident occurred was not one of the regular pay-as-you-enter cars with doors that draw up the steps and close tightly, but was one of the old cars worked over, with the conductor at the rear end taking up fares. This caused a congestion in this part of the car and prevented all the children from getting safely into the car before it started. Had the modern up-to-date car been used, or proper care shown by the conductor, no accident would have occurred.

    I am sending you the last number of the High School Magazine which was issued as a memorial number.

    You will be surprised, and I have no doubt will be pleased, to learn that I expect to start for South America about the first of June, going by way of Panama to Lima, Valparaiso, Santiago, Mendoza, and back by way of La Paz, making, of course, numerous intermediate stops. I am going primarily and almost wholly in the interest of my Cactus Investigation, and hope to make large collections in all these western deserts. I do not know how long I shall be away, but certainly not less than 3 months, possibly 5 or 6. Mrs. Rose will go with me and help me in my photography and collecting generally. She needs the change, and I think it will do her good.

Yours very truly,

J.N. Rose

Research Associate.

CARNEGIE INSTITUTION OF WASHINGTON
DEPARTMENT OF BOTANICAL RESEARCH

COASTAL LABORATORY, CARMEL, CALIFORNIA   DESERT LABORATORY, TUCSON, ARIZONA

Smithsonian Institution, Washington, D. C.,
April 23, 1914.

Mr. Walter Deane,
    29 Brewster Street,
        Cambridge, Massachusetts.

My dear Mr. Deane:

        I think I told you that I hope to get off to South America soon after the first of June. One of the places on my proposed itinerary is Arequipa, Peru, where Harvard University has an observatory. I believe that Professor Campbell is in charge, but whether he is there or not I do not know. Are you acquainted with any of the people stationed at Arequipa?

        Yours very truly,

        J. N. Rose
        Research Associate.

CARNEGIE INSTITUTION OF WASHINGTON
DEPARTMENT OF BOTANICAL RESEARCH

COASTAL LABORATORY, CARMEL, CALIFORNIA   DESERT LABORATORY, TUCSON, ARIZONA

Smithsonian Institution, Washington, D. C.,

May 16, 1914.

Mr. Walter Deane,
    29 Brewster Street,
        Cambridge, Massachusetts.

My dear Mr. Deane:

        I have just received a very nice letter, as well as a letter of introduction to Professor Campbell, from Mr. Pickering.

    Our plans are moving along very nicely for our proposed trip, and we hope now to leave New York on the 10th of June.

                              Yours very truly,

                                            Research Associate.

Rec'd Jun 24/14

HOTEL WASHINGTON COLON R.P.

June 19/914

My dear Deane:

We had a most delightful trip, with a day at Kingston where we visited the Hope Botanical Gardens.

Mrs. Rose was well the whole trip and did not miss a single meal.

Mr. Pittier met us at Colon. We are stopping for a day at this beautiful hotel which over hangs the waters of the bay. Tonight we go on to Panama City where we will spend several days.

We both send love. Your friend

Rose

TARJETA POSTAL

CARTE POSTALE – POSTKARTE – POST CARD

Frau Emma Müller jr. Lima, Peru.

Aug 17/1917

Luis Sablich, Callao, Perú.

Puente de Viscas. (F. C. C. del Perú.)

TARJETA POSTAL
CARTE POSTALE   POSTKARTE - POST CARD

From Lms. J. N. Rose from Lima Peru.
July 17, 1914.
W.D.

CARNEGIE INSTITUTION OF WASHINGTON
DEPARTMENT OF BOTANICAL RESEARCH

COASTAL LABORATORY CARMEL, CALIFORNIA   DESERT LABORATORY, TUCSON, ARIZONA

Smithsonian Institution, Washington, D. C.,

December 19, 1914.

Mr. Walter Deane,
    29 Brewster Street,
        Cambridge, Massachusetts.

My dear Deane:

    Please pardon me for not answering your various kind letters and telegram since my return home. I have been dreadfully rushed ever since I landed in America. In fact, Dr. Britton sent me a wireless off Cape Hatteras asking me to stop off to see him on my way home, and I have been on the go ever since. Last week I went out to Liberty to see my mother and start her off for a winter in California, and I am just back at my desk again.

    Yes, Joseph was married on Thanksgiving Day to Miss Dorothy Cray, a very charming young lady. Her father is the District Judge in our part of the State, and an uncle is a Member of Congress.

    Mrs. Rose and I are going up to Philadelphia on the 28th, to attend some of the meetings of the American Association for the Advancement of Science and of the Botanical Society of America. I wish you and Mrs. Deane were to be there.

    We met so many nice people in Peru, Bolivia and Chile, and I only wish I had time to tell you something about my trip.

    I am glad that you enjoyed the Times article.

Mrs. Rose and I slipped into New York and went to the MacAlpin Hotel, where we supposed no one knew us; but as we came into the hotel about midnight from a walk about Fifth Avenue, a bunch of newspaper men held me up and would not let me free until I told them about my trip and gave them a few scientific names--just to make their stuff sound good, they said.

                    Yours very truly,

                    Research Associate.

P. S.

    Someone has sent me a card with reference to Doctor Farlow's birthday yesterday, and although a little late, I sent off my letter yesterday. Let me know how the thing went off, and who was at the bottom of this. It is certainly a splendid idea and I am glad to help it along.

CARNEGIE INSTITUTION OF WASHINGTON
DEPARTMENT OF BOTANICAL RESEARCH

COASTAL LABORATORY, CARMEL, CALIFORNIA   DESERT LABORATORY, TUCSON, ARIZONA

Smithsonian Institution, Washington, D. C.,

January 2/, 1915.

Mr. Walter Deane,
    29 Brewster Street,
        Cambridge, Massachusetts.

My dear Deane:

Your letter came to hand last night and we were all very glad indeed to hear from you. Yes, I have been very busy since my return from South America, trying to get my collection properly mounted, my notes put into shape, and the like. I brought back with me more than a thousand numbers, and, of course, a great many things besides the Cactuses, such as mosses, ferns, senecios for Greenman, grasses for Hitchcock, and the like.

When in Chile I obtained a set of the Chilean stamps from one cent up to one dollar, and this I am enclosing in this letter.

You wrote to Mrs. Rose some time ago that you and Mrs. Deane might come to see us some time during early spring. We shall be very glad to have you come whenever convenient for you. April is a lovely month here.

Doctor Britton wishes me to go to South America about the first of May, but I hardly think I can get away by that time.

Yours very truly,

JNRose

CARNEGIE INSTITUTION OF WASHINGTON
DEPARTMENT OF BOTANICAL RESEARCH

COASTAL LABORATORY, CARMEL, CALIFORNIA   DESERT LABORATORY, TUCSON, ARIZONA

Smithsonian Institution, Washington, D. C.,

January 28, 1915.

Mr. Walter Deane,
    29 Brewster Street,
        Cambridge, Massachusetts.

My dear Mr. Deane:

        I came back from New York Monday night and found your very kind letter awaiting me. I am sorry to hear that you have been sick, but I trust that you are now quite well again.

    With regard to the stamps, please do not think of paying for them. In fact, I have not the least recollection of the amount; at the most it was only a trifle. This you can readily understand when I tell you that my common tip to the dining room waiter was 5 pesos.

    I think it will be better to give the entire set to one person, as the set is complete as far as it goes, and it will be too bad to break it. I find that George has some other duplicates and these I am enclosing, along with a Peruvian dollar stamp, which I think some one of your young friends will find very interesting.

                              Yours very truly,

CARNEGIE INSTITUTION OF WASHINGTON
DEPARTMENT OF BOTANICAL RESEARCH

COASTAL LABORATORY CARMEL, CALIFORNIA   DESERT LABORATORY, TUCSON, ARIZONA

Smithsonian Institution, Washington, D. C.,

March 5, 1915.

Mr. Walter Deane,
    29 Brewster Street,
        Cambridge, Massachusetts.

My dear Deane:

Your very good letter came to us on March the 2nd. We are all very much delighted that you are coming on this spring. The date for your coming will suit us very well; but the date for your departure, I would suggest that you leave open and decide after you have come to Washington.

Mrs. Rose will write in a day or two.

Yours hastily,

J. A. Rose

CARNEGIE INSTITUTION OF WASHINGTON
DEPARTMENT OF BOTANICAL RESEARCH

COASTAL LABORATORY, CARMEL, CALIFORNIA   DESERT LABORATORY, TUCSON, ARIZONA

Smithsonian Institution, Washington, D. C.,
April 6, 1915.

Mr. Walter Deane,
    29 Brewster Street,
        Cambridge, Massachusetts.

My dear Deane:

    I am getting out of the city to-night* at midnight, but shall be back in time to see you in Washington on Friday.

    We are all delighted to know that you are to be here so soon. Our dreadful storm of Saturday has all gone, and the weather now is very pleasant again.

        Yours very truly,

Dictated [*Monday], but not signed by   J. N. Rose.
                                        Per Wm. R. Fitch.

CARNEGIE INSTITUTION OF WASHINGTON
DEPARTMENT OF BOTANICAL RESEARCH

COASTAL LABORATORY, CARMEL, CALIFORNIA   DESERT LABORATORY, TUCSON, ARIZONA

Smithsonian Institution, Washington, D. C.,
May 1, 1915.

Mr. Walter Deane,
    29 Brewster Street,
        Cambridge, Massachusetts.

My dear Mr. Deane:

    Your various cards and letters have been received and have been greatly appreciated by all the family. I am very busy, as you can well understand, making my final arrangements for my departure from New York a week from to-day.

    Doctor Greene told me that he was sending you some of his book plates the other day, and I am now sending you five copies of the John Donnell Smith collection.

    Mr. Russell has your plants in shape and they will be sent to you in a day or two.

    Mr. Fairchild has just published in his Plant Immigrants a beautiful picture of the Ginkgo Avenue in the Department of Agriculture grounds, and I am asking him to send a copy of this report to you so that you can get a copy of this photograph.

    I am having a copy of Mr. Maxon's report on my South American ferns sent to you, and I am also enclosing some extracts from the Bulletin of the New York Botanical Garden.

                Yours very truly,

                        Research Associate.

EXCERPTS FROM THE BULLETIN OF THE NEW YORK BOTANICAL GARDEN VOLUME 9

(Issued March 31, 1915)

Report of the Director-in-Chief for the year 1914

Exploration

The most important exploration trip accomplished was that of Dr. and Mrs. J. N. Rose to Peru, Bolivia, and Chile for the collection of cacti, in continuation of cooperation with the Carnegie Institution of Washington in the study of these plants. They visited the desert regions of these countries and obtained living plants and museum and herbarium specimens of most of the many kinds of cacti which grow there, and these collections have all been received at the Garden, for the most part in capital condition forming the most important addition to our cactus collections ever made on a single expedition. The Garden's cooperation in this work was effected through an appropriation from the income of the Darius Ogden Mills Fund.

Administration and Organization

Such time as I have had for scientific investigation has been given to the continuation of the cactus investigation in cooperation with Drs. D. T. MacDougal and J. N. Rose, of the Carnegie Institution of Washington, to studies of the West Indian flora, and to assisting Mr. Norman Taylor in his production of the forthcoming flora of the vicinity of New York City.

Report by Dr. F. H. Rusby on the Economic Collections

Through the expedition of Dr. J. N. Rose, of the National Herbarium, to the west coast of South America, we have obtained a number of very rare food products. In addition to the samples of foods themselves, Dr. Rose has supplied living roots of the plants yielding them, which are now growing luxuriantly in our economic plant collection.

Report of the Chairman of the Scientific Directors, Dr. H. H. Rusby

First in importance, probably, is the expedition to the West Andean region, for the study and collection of Cactaceae, undertaken in cooperation with the Carnegie Institution of Washington and the United States Department of Agriculture. This work has been executed as proposed to you in our last report, except that Dr. J. N. Rose, of the National Herbarium, who is associated with Dr. Britton in this study, found it possible to make the journey himself, instead of sending Dr. Shafer. Mrs. Rose accompanied and assisted her husband in his difficult and laborious undertaking. The results, from a scientific standpoint, are of the richest description. It is believed that most of the species of Cactaceae growing on the Pacific side of the Andes are now represented in our collection, both in the dried and growing condition. Most of these species have not previously been known in cultivation. Some of them, and probably one or more genera, are new to science. We take great satisfaction in the receipt of this splendid addition to our collections, especially in view of its usefulness in contributing to the monograph of the family, upon which we are now engaged.

morning and we felt very
lonely without you and this
evening only Mrs. Rose and I
sat down stairs to talk while
the children were at church.
The weather is cool and lovely.
The girls and I are invited to
a musicale at Mrs. Lewis'
May 11th to meet some relatives
who have settled near the Lewis'.
I saw Mrs. S. yesterday and she
was as cordial and nice.
As the time approaches for Mrs.
Rose's departure my heart gets heavier
and heavier. It seems so terrible —
heart-breaking that he should go off
alone and leave me behind.
But I have used up the space — so I
must say good night — [illegible] love to you both

My dear Deane:
    Your little box came
yesterday and was opened with
a great deal of interest. You
must forgive me when I tell
you it brought tears to my
eyes. How many times have
I opened your packages with
the dear dear boy that is gone!
Your little knife is a real
beauty and I shall always
think of you when I use
it. This afternoon I took it

line, Pier 8 Brooklyn N.Y.
We are all quite well
but we miss the Deans
so very much.
Give our dearest love
to Mrs Deen. Your friend
May 2/1915   J. Rose

Dear Mr. Dean,
I see Mr. Rose has left a space
it seems a pity to send so
much blank paper!
The knife is a dear, just like
the giver. We miss you both so
much. We all went to church this

with me when Mr Rose & George
& I took a little walk into the
woods beyond the Calvert Street
Bridge. The woods are
beautiful with the leaves nearly
fully grown.
It has been cool & lovely today.
We all went to church today
as usual.
I leave here Friday morning.
Will be at the McAlpin
Hotel Friday night &
Sail Saturday on the
S.S. Tennyson, Lamport & Holt

CARNEGIE INSTITUTION OF WASHINGTON
DEPARTMENT OF BOTANICAL RESEARCH

COASTAL LABORATORY, CARMEL, CALIFORNIA   DESERT LABORATORY, TUCSON, ARIZONA

Smithsonian Institution, Washington, D. C.,
May 4, 1915.

Mr. Walter Deane,
    29 Brewster Street,
        Cambridge, Massachusetts.

My dear Mr. Deane:

I am enclosing a copy of the itinerary for my coming trip. I am also sending you, under separate cover, a copy of "A Synopsis of Mexican and Central American Umbelliferae."

Yours very truly,

J. N. Rose
Research Associate.

SMITHSONIAN INSTITUTION
UNITED STATES NATIONAL MUSEUM
WASHINGTON, D. C.

May 6, 1915.

Mr. Walter Deane,
   29 Brewster Street,
      Cambridge, Massachusetts.

My dear Mr. Deane:

      I am sending you under Museum frank 3 specimens which are intended as an exchange for plants which you stated you would be glad to collect for us next year.

      Yours very truly,

      Associate in Botany.

Hotel McAlpin
Greeley Square
New York City

1681

MERRY & BOOMER,
MANAGERS

My dear Mr. Deane:

I left Washington at 10:03 this morning. Mrs. Rowe is heartbroken and now this Louisiana tragedy has added to her worry. I have just had a wire asking if it was safe for me to go tomorrow. I leave at 11:00 A.M. Mr. Russell is here with me.

I took dinner with Dr. Butler

*Rec'd in Shelburne NH
June 22 —*

Bahia, Brazil
May 25 /1915

My dear Deane:

Here we are at last in Bahia after sixteen days at sea. The trip was long and uninteresting. The people onboard as a rule were common businessmen, salesmen & the like and I am sorry to say many of them were rotten.

We landed in Bahia about 10 & soon found a "Pensão Ingleza" where we have two nice rooms & good board for which we pay 20,000 reis per day!!

Before my baggage came indeed within a half hour after finding rooms I went out on the hill overlooking the bay & found a Cactus which I cut off with your knife & brought home. It may require a new name. It was collected by Velloso in 1785 but wrongly called Cactus triangularis!

3

six species in the lot. There are said to be 12 species in Bahia and are shelled by the thousands.

He collected 6 species of sea weeds and took 3 photos showing how it grows on the rocks & is washed by the waves.

You see we are having a great time for I am dead tired and much closer.

I miss Mrs Rice for it was no trip for her to take.

My love to Mrs Deane.

Your friend
Moore

So you see the work is starting off well. This is our second day and we have 20 numbers & have seen 6 species of Cactus. Only 19 have been reported from the state. Bahia, the state is nearly as large as Germany. The city has 300000 people at least 90 percent of whom are colored.

On Saturday we will go into the interior for 2 weeks.

I found your very good letter in New York & "No 2" here in Bahia this afternoon. I wish you were here with me. What a time we would have. I am finding all kind of interesting plants. 2 mosses were taken today for Williams (see the May or June Bull. Torr. Club for his report on my west coast), two plants for Dr. Pearson, & 4 toad stools for Dr. Murrill. I am remembering all my friends.

I bought 10 humming birds for Ivereson to mount. They are beautifully prepared. I think there are

My dear Dane:

Letters 3 & 4 came today. It is well for this is the only free day I have had since we reached Bahia. We spent a week in and about Bahia & then went to the desert on the northern border of the state, about 300 miles north of here. It took us 2 days to make the trip! Oh what a country — & what a people!! About 90% of the people are black or part black. We first passed through the heavily wooded coast region & finally came out onto the open grassy country & at last reached the deserts or caatinga where the trees & shrubs are low, mostly & spiny. Catinga or Caatinga is an Indian work (meaning "see far." Here we found many Cacti and brought back 14 boxes which we are shipping off tomorrow!

I met a Dr. Zehntner who had a very nice little collection of 26 native species. These we described, photographed or brought back with us.

2

I had expected to go on to Rio after making this trip but Dr. Z. tells me about some strange species in the Southern part of the State 80 M.R. & I will leave again Tuesday for a week or two & will then come back & leave for the South.

The Cacti are more interesting here than I had expected. Schumann referred about 12 species to Bahia. There are probably 45 species some new. I have two new genera!

I had several letters from home. Poor Mrs. Rose is heartbroken over my leaving.

Give my dearest love to Mrs Deane.

Your friend

J.N. Rose

June 13/15

RMS "AVON"
July 5 /15

My dear Jane:

At last we are through our work at Bahia and are now on this beautiful ship on our way to Rio. We shipped 2 stores of plants from Bahia and one of the finest collections I have ever made

can get home if I stay limited I spent all my money. At one little town we met a Canadian who invited us to stop with him but when he left the next day he turned over his house & man & lest us in charge. We paid all bills for food etc. This amounted to 5 crowns per day! (1.25 American). The house was clean, the food good and a fine bath every morning! Mr Shirrell had collected several hundred beetles. Will write ser-

We have over 40 living species of Cacti, many mosses, ferns & the like — in fact about 600 numbers in all.
In the dense tropical forest I found a tree 45 feet high a new species of Opuntia!
Our trips into the heart of the state of Bahia were pretty hard. I was dreadfully punished by insects & cacti spines and could not sleep at

all one night. I had a dreadful experience one night with ants.
On one of our boat trips we met — a very distinguished botanist Prof. C. Torrend. You may recall Lloyds Sketch of him & mycological notes about [?] 1911.
He is making big collections here.
The R.R. people were very kind and gave us all kinds of favors stuffed my specimens full & sent them when I

I am now this
Friday noon doing
still work to Rio.
may not go further.
Making great collection

Mr Walter Deane
Cambridge
Mass
United States of America
29 Brewster Street.

R.M.S.P. "ARAGUAYA"

My dear Deane:

At last I have come to a place where I can stop and think of my friends. I am on a ship going to Argentina. I have just spent six delightful weeks at Rio de Janeiro.

Our collection numbers over 1200 mostly Cacti, ferns & mosses. We have now shipped to N.Y. Botanical Garden 75 boxes large & small. The Brazilian Government has been very kind sending me on all kinds of trips always with one of its botanists and paying all transportation charges while only leaving the tips for me. I have been to Cabo Frio, Itatiaya (the highest mountain in Brazil)

It was however one continual rush from early morn to late at night. There was so much to see, so much to do, and so little time.

Rio is the most inland -ing place in the world. Our hotel the International Hotel is in the center of the city, and yet the region there about, is as wild as on Mt. Washington.

We were located on the side of Corcovado, nearly 1000 ft alt. where we could see the entrance to the Harbor, all the shipping the most beautiful view I have ever seen. At our back was the forest primeval — All kinds of beautiful ferns, tall tree ferns & delicate little maiden hairs. The trees were all festooned with species of Cacti (Rhipsalis) of which I have seen about 30 species mostly from Rio.

R.M.S.P. "ARAGUAYA."

São Paulo, the second city in Brazil, Petropolis, Ihla Grande and have visited most of the high mountains about Rio.

The Botanical Garden at Rio is very beautiful. It is over 100 years old. It has a wonderful collection of palms – 230 species growing in the open.

Your last letter was number 7. Good one too.

I have spent so much time in Brazil that I will have little time for Argentina.

I hope to leave for the U.S. about the 16th of September.

Give my dearest love to Mrs Dearme;

Your friend
J.J.Pie

Aug. 20/1915 –

ans
Oct 14/15

Emilio Levy
Teléfono N° 104

Grand Hotel
Plaza San Martin

Mendoza, Sept. 3 de 1915

My dear Deane:

We left Buenos Aires Monday afternoon & reached Mendoza the next afternoon – a 25 hour trip. Mendoza lies at the foot of the Andes on the west side of Argentina. It is an interesting trip across Argentina. The eastern part is very fertile & suggests Illinois while the west is very dry like Arizona. Indeed I can hardly tell it from Arizona for you have the Acacia, the Palo Verde, the Larrea (I find 4 species of Larrea in Mendoza!) the Opuntia & other similar Cacti, etc, etc.

I met here Mr. Reed who was with Prof. Hoxter in Chile. – He is a most delightful man. He is now packing a big box of bird skins for me to take back to Ridgway.

On Thursday we went up into the mountains where we found all kinds of interesting Cacti. Mendoza is especially interesting to me for the first Cacti from Argentina were sent from Mendoza and many of them have been described again & again.

Emilio Levy
Teléfono N.º 104

Grand Hotel
Plaza San Martin

Mendoza, _____ de 191__

We have about 20 species from here and will send back tomorrow six boxes of living plants.

It is very dry at Mendoza. Some years they have only 3 mm. of rain during a whole year!

It is the grape country of Argentina. You see miles & miles of vineyards. Wine is cheaper than water in the hotels!

My work is now nearly finished and I shall soon start home.

Give my dearest love to Mrs. Deane & believe me,

Your friend
J. N. Rose

Rec'd Oct 8.

Cordoba, ~~Sept.~~ 11 de 1915

My dear Deane:

We came up to Cordoba last ~~Monday~~ night and have used this as a base going as far as ~~Cruz~~ Jesús Maria & Casse ffuith. We are ~~taking~~ back ~~with~~ us 4 boxes of living Cacti. Here is located a great University and an observatory. I met Dr. Kurtz who wants to be remembered to ~~Dr.~~ Dr Robinson & Miss Day.

Please ~~ex~~ use this hasty note.

Your friend

JN Rose

CARNEGIE INSTITUTION OF WASHINGTON
DEPARTMENT OF BOTANICAL RESEARCH

DESERT LABORATORY, TUCSON, ARIZONA

Smithsonian Institution, Washington, D. C.,

October 13, 1915.

Mr. Walter Deane,
    29 Brewster Street,
        Cambridge, Massachusetts.

My dear Mr. Deane:

        I have been intending to write to you ever since I returned to Washington a week ago to-day, but you can well understand that I have been rather busy. Our collection, consisting of about 1700 numbers, is all here to be arranged and made ready for mounting. In addition to this I brought back from Mendoza over a hundred birds, snaked, reptiles, a large collection of diatoms, more than 300 mosses, fully 300 ferns, shells and in fact all kinds of natural history material. Mr. Russell collected some 200 beetles and these I am writing to Professor Thaxter about. These will go through the ordinary Museum channels. I purchased a small collection on my own hook and this I am sending to him to look over.

    Mrs. Rose and I leave for New York this afternoon and will be at the McAlpin Hotel for the remainder of the week.

    Just as soon as I can get time I shall write to you more about my trip.

    I enclose a bulletin which you will be interested in looking over.

                                Yours very truly,

                                Rose

CARNEGIE INSTITUTION OF WASHINGTON
DEPARTMENT OF BOTANICAL RESEARCH

COASTAL LABORATORY, CARMEL, CALIFORNIA DESERT LABORATORY, TUCSON, ARIZONA

Smithsonian Institution, Washington, D. C.,
November 27, 1915.

Mr. Walter Deane,
 29 Brewster Street,
  Cambridge, Massachusetts.

My dear Mr. Deane:

Please pardon me for not having written to you sooner, but I have been very much occupied since I came home. I have been in New York four times since October 6th and may go once or twice more before the opening of the new year.

I read a paper before the National Academy in New York on the 17th of this month.

I have had several nice letters from Professor Thaxter. I met several people who collected with him in South America, and he has told me who it was that published on his pets so soon after he came back!

I have just had a nice letter from Oakes Ames, who, as you probably know, is leaving for South America very soon.

Yours very truly,

Research Associate.

CARNEGIE INSTITUTION OF WASHINGTON
DEPARTMENT OF BOTANICAL RESEARCH

DESERT LABORATORY, TUCSON, ARIZONA

Smithsonian Institution, Washington, D. C.,

March 30, 1916.

Mr. Walter Deane,

    29 Brewster Street,

        Cambridge, Massachusetts.

My dear Mr. Deane:

    Your letter of March 13 came duly to hand, and we were delighted to hear from you. Pardon me for not writing sooner about the photographs. They are very attractive and I shall have them mounted and put into the Herbarium collection as coming from your brother. I should certainly be very glad to have one of the enlarged photographs, but I do not want to put you to the expense of framing it.

    Yours very truly,

    JA Coe

    Research Associate.

Hotel Belmont
**FORTY-SECOND ST.
AT PARK AVENUE**
CABLE ADDRESS "MONTBEL" (OPPOSITE GRAND CENTRAL TERMINAL)

H. I. M. HATES.

New York

My dear Dave:

The picture was very interesting and Mrs. Rose says it shall have a good place on the walls. He took it down to have it framed the days I came up here.

Mrs. Britton wanted to know what word we had from you,

Hotel Belmont
FORTY-SECOND ST. AT PARK AVENUE
(OPPOSITE GRAND CENTRAL TERMINAL)

CABLE ADDRESS "MONTBEL"

New York

2

The Book is coming along — one part will soon be done.

I had a nice little visit with Dr. Robinson last week.

Give our love to Mrs. Dane.

Your friend,

J. [signature]

April 13/16

CARNEGIE INSTITUTION OF WASHINGTON
DEPARTMENT OF BOTANICAL RESEARCH

COASTAL LABORATORY, CARMEL, CALIFORNIA   DESERT LABORATORY, TUCSON, ARIZONA

Smithsonian Institution, Washington, D. C.,
September 30, 1916.

Mr. Walter Deane,
   29 Brewster Street,
      Cambridge, Massachusetts.

My dear Deane:

      I have been hoping to write to you to tell you that I am going to South America once more; but you can well understand that I have had very little time at my disposal. We* sail on the Red "D" Line S. S. CARACAS Wednesday at one p. m., stopping first at Porto Rico, then at Curacao, at both places only for short times, and then on to Caracas, which will be our base. Letters addressed to us care of the American Consul, Caracas, Venezuela, will reach us.

                Very truly yours,

                          Research Associate.

* Mrs. Rose and I.

CARNEGIE INSTITUTION OF WASHINGTON
DEPARTMENT OF BOTANICAL RESEARCH

DESERT LABORATORY, TUCSON, ARIZONA

April 25, 1918.

My dear Mr. Deane:

Rebecca handed me your letter of March 25, to look up the little umble from Plummer Island but I have not had a minute to do it until this very moment. I recall very well the day the plant was collected and I have a duplicate in the National Herbarium. I am sending you an autograph label which you may keep if you desire. I do have some confusion about my initials. As you know, there is a botanist writer in New York whose initials are N. J. and our names come together in Bailey's Encyclopedia, in his list of contributors.

By the way speaking of Bailey, I saw him, yesterday at the meetings of the National Academy and we were talking about you and your birthday. You know Bailey was elected a member of the National Academy, last year and this was his first attendance at the meeting of this august body. He must have felt rather lonesome as he was the only out-of-town botanist who attended the meeting.

You have perhaps noticed by the papers that Professor Atkinson was elected a member at the meeting yesterday.

A much more able botanist but perhaps not so well known failed of election.

Speaking of birthdays my old friend and neighbor, General Wilcox, who comes to see me at least once a week, tells me that he will celebrate his seventy-eighth birthday, to-morrow.

I am just back from New York where I have been in conference with Dr. Britton on the third part of our cactus book. The first part is now in page proof, the second in the editor's hands and the third is nearly complete.

Yours very truly,

JN Rose

SMITHSONIAN INSTITUTION
UNITED STATES NATIONAL MUSEUM
WASHINGTON, D. C.

July 22, 1918.

Mr. Walter Deane,
 Philbrook Farm,
  Shelbourne, New Hampshire.

My dear Deane:

    George and I are starting for Ecuador, to-day, and so I can now write you a brief note. I have been planning to write this letter for more than a month but, somehow or other, my plans would not mature. Everything is now ready. We are looking forward to a most profitable journey over the high mountains of Ecuador, made famous by Humboldt, Spruce and others. I suppose that you have already read Spruce's "Travels on the Amazon and in the Andes", a most delightful book as you very well know. You will probably enjoy reading the second volume now that I am traveling over his old route.

    Mrs. Rose and the girls will keep you informed as to my movements. I fear that I will have little time to write to my friends as there is so much to do and my time is so limited.

    Your picture has been a great delight to us. It is a very fine reproduction. Thank you very, very much for it.

    I am enclosing a copy of my itinerary, which, however, is subject to change.   Very sincerely, *J. N. Rose*

rec'd at
Shelburne N.H.
Sept. 27, 1918

Huigra Ecuador,
Aug 28, 1918.

My dear Deane:
George and I returned here to our Ecuadorean home yesterday and found your good letter awaiting us. We are surely having a great time botanically. I am busy all the time, too busy to write — but I must jot down a few lines to you. I am glad you are going to read Spruce. He too is one of the classics. If you read him I need not describe the country for I am going over his route & all about which he has described so well. Yesterday we came down from Sibambe [?] over the route described by him (Vol.2 p. 228-237). With his book in hand we left Ambato, crossed the shoulder of the mighty Chimborazo at an altitude of 11,500 ft., went to Riobamba, passed through Guamote, Ticsan & Alausi and Chuchi while Lucmas can be seen from our hotel. We saw the hedges of Yucca and "Aguve" although it is not a yucca, collected Hedyotis, collected also the "succulent Composita" (a Senecio) and saw the "silky-leaved Montage". I can tell you this was interesting. Next week we are to go down below Lucmas to collect the Cinchona or redbark!

There is much more that I could tell you about this trip if I only had the time. We are making large collections and are finding many strange plants some of which must be new! For example I find 4 very distinct species of of Carica. I collected 2 species of Tropeolum this morning. I am finding some strange Cacti. It is a most interesting flora. I want to tell you more about it but must close.

Yours [sincerely?]
[signature]

I have not yet written Dr Robinson but I have him in mind [surely?] for Tropoleum and its allies are very abundant and I am trying not to let any of them get by me. We shall start for Southern Ecuador in about 10 days.

SMITHSONIAN INSTITUTION
UNITED STATES NATIONAL MUSEUM
WASHINGTON, D. C.

August 24, 1919.

Mr. Walter Deane,
    Philbrook Farm,
        Shelbourne, New Hampshire.

My dear Mr. Deane:

    Your very good letter of August 8 was forwarded to me in New York where I was spending ten days with Dr. Britton reading the proof of our second Cactus volume. I came home a week ago today. While in New York I also read the proof of a little account of my trip to Ecuador which is soon to appear in the Journal of the New York Botanical Garden.

    Yes, I am certainly glad to have this first Cactus volume finished. Unfortunately, I have practically no copies to distributed and the price of the volume is going to prevent its coming into the hands of many people whom I should like to have have it. The first volume sells for eighteen dollars and, of course, I am not able to buy any presentation copies. I had a letter the other day from a correspondent, an amateur in Cacti, enclosing a check for eighteen dollars, and asking me to autograph the copy which I sent to him, a rather unusual proceeding it seems to me.

    I am just writing a letter to the Editor of Science who has asked me to indicate the names of twenty botanists worthy to be starred in the next edition of AMERICAN MEN OF SCIENCE. It give me great pleasure to suggest your name.

    Your note saying that you were collecting white violets reminds me that I collected some very, very interesting red violets last year. I have just had a report from Dr. Britton saying that I have three species.

                      Very truly,

                       J. N. Rose

SMITHSONIAN INSTITUTION
UNITED STATES NATIONAL MUSEUM
WASHINGTON, D. C.

August 27, 1920.

Mr. Walter Deane,
    Philbrook Farm,
        Shelbourne, New Hampshire.

My dear Mr. Deane:

  Your letter of April 24 has remained unanswered too long. A few days ago I received a letter from you which recalled the fact that I had neglected you. Fortunately, however, this letter was intended for my good wife but it did remind me that I must at once write you as I had long wanted to do.

  Now that my second cactus volume is off the press - I read the last proof yesterday and it will be soon distributed - I have one less care. The third volume, though, must go to press before very long and then there will be another year of proof reading of plates and manuscript. This second volume is going to be very attractive. It contains eight more plates than Volume I and these are much more varied and showy.

  I was very much disappointed that I could not go to South America this year as I had made all my plans and was looking forward to making a great collection of cacti in Brazil and Argentina. Perhaps it is best that I did not go for travel conditions have been very bad between New York and South America. I have had my hands full, however, with all kinds of interesting problems. Besides my cactus work I have been doing intensive work on the flora of Ecuador and have found new species and genera without number.

SMITHSONIAN INSTITUTION
UNITED STATES NATIONAL MUSEUM
WASHINGTON, D. C.

Mr. Deane   -2-   8/27/1920

    One of our men here is just back from Haiti where he spent the last six months making a general collection. He has brought back some very interesting cacti for me, one of which I am just now studying; this was collected by Plumier but has never been identified since his time. It is a tree thirty feet high.

    I see by the papers that the Ornithological Union is to have its meeting here this fall. Can you not come down to this meeting? We want to extend to you a very cordial invitation to make our home your headquarters. You can go to the meetings just as little as you want to. Write to us at once that we may expect you. My plans are such that I will be here this fall. The whole family will welcome you. Unfortunately George will be at Princeton but I have no doubt that he will come down over Sunday to see you.

                Very truly,

SMITHSONIAN INSTITUTION
UNITED STATES NATIONAL MUSEUM
WASHINGTON, D. C.

May 17, 1921

rec'd
May 18

Mr. Walter Deane,
29 Brewster Street,
Cambridge, Massachusetts.

My dear Deane:

Dr. Blake told me a few days ago that he had seen you in Cambridge recently and how much he had enjoyed seeing you again. I have been intending to write you for a long time, but somehow I have kept putting it off from week to week. Mrs. Rose was afraid that you might be sick again as it has been so long since we have had any word from you.

Rebecca and Martha have just returned from a week's visit in Princeton. George is just closing his Junior year. He is looking forward to entering Harvard Law School as soon as he gets through Princeton. My mother has spent the winter with us and is planning to leave next week for her home in Indiana.

I expect to go to New York next Monday for a few days with Dr. Britton to work upon the fourth volume which is well advanced. The third volume was turned over to Mr. Barnum last January, but owing to the congested condition of the office, the volume is still in the editor's hands. Just now however he is at work upon the illustrations and we hope soon to see proof of it.

I am to-day reading proof of a little paper which the Smithsonian is publishing for me on a remarkable Cactus from Haiti. This plant was first collected by Plumier about 1696. It was overlooked by Linneus, made the type of a new species in the genus Cactus by Lamarck and referred to the genus Cereus by De Candolle, but no one has collected good material of it until 1920 when one of our collectors here rediscovered the plant. It is one of the largest and most curious of all the

Mr. Deane   -2-   May 17, 1921

plants in this family.

I was very much delighted to see that Dr. Robinson was elected a member of the National Academy a few weeks ago.

This has been a very interesting spring on account of the many scientific gatherings and receptions which have been held. A few weeks ago a delightful reception was given the Secretary of State and Mrs. Hughes at the Pan American Building. Then we had the reception to the Prince of Monaco, a brief address from Einstein and this week we are to have a reception to Madame Curie. These have all been extremely enjoyable.

We are all quite well. We shall be glad to hear from you when you can take the time to write.

Very truly,

SMITHSONIAN INSTITUTION
UNITED STATES NATIONAL MUSEUM
WASHINGTON, D. C.

February 10, 1922.

Mr. Walter Deane;
29 Brewster Street,
Cambridge, Massachusetts.

My dear Mr. Deane:

    Your letter of December 31, 1921, is before me; in fact it has been before me ever since it was received but I have been so much engrossed with proof-reading and other things that I have neglected not only you but other correspondents.

    We received your Christmas present several days before Christmas and strictly followed your injunction and did not open it until Christmas Morning. I want to thank you most heartily for remembering us.

    I said that I had been busy with proof-reading and the like. My cactus volume, volume 3, has long been in proof but owing to the delays in having the colored illustrations made it has been held up much longer than we had hoped. Rebecca and I have read carefully three proofs of it and there is one more

SMITHSONIAN INSTITUTION
UNITED STATES NATIONAL MUSEUM
WASHINGTON, D. C.

Mr. Deane   -2-   February 10, 1922.

to be read and a long index is to be made. Volume 4 has nearly all been written and I am planning to turn it in to the Carnegie Institution on the first of April. It will however take a year or more to get it through the press.

George is finishing his senior year at Princeton. He will be home to-morrow for his mid-year vacation. He hopes to enter Harvard Law School in the fall and is looking forward to seeing you frequently. Perhaps Mrs. Rose and I will get up to Cambridge while George is there. In fact, I suggested to George that we attend the American Association meeting at Cambridge but he prefers to spend Christmas at home. We are all quite well at home and very often talk of you and every now and then someone brings word that they have seen you. I think the last Washington man who was back from Cambridge is Eggleston.

Last night we attended the Congressional Reception at the White House at which it is stated that more

Mr. Deane — -2- — February 10, 1922.

than three thousand were present. Of the six people in the receiving line four were from Massachusetts. Mrs. Rose wore the beautiful black dress of Mrs. Deane. She looked very handsome.

    I am just sending a little note on the rediscovery of Coelopleurum actaeifolium on Long Island to Torreya. I suppose that you have plants from New York.

    Very truly,

    J N Rose

SMITHSONIAN INSTITUTION
UNITED STATES NATIONAL MUSEUM
WASHINGTON, D. C.

September 20, 1922

Mr. Walter Deane,
   29 Brewster Street,
      Cambridge, Massachusetts.

My dear Mr. Deane:

    George has already written you that he is leaving for Cambridge next Friday and that he is looking forward to a most profitable and interesting year in the Harvard Law School. You will doubtless see him from time to time and will find him a delightful and interesting boy.

    We all spent two weeks at Atlantic City and are now back home once more.

    I think that I told you that my cactus work was being brought to a close. My third volume has all been printed but unfortunately there is delay in getting the plates out so that the volume has not yet been issued. The fourth volume is in manuscript with many beautiful illustrations but it will be more than a year before it is actually off the press.

    I hope that you have had a delightful summer and that I shall hear from you before long. I have given Mr. Ivan M. Johnston a letter to you which he will probably present at the herbarium sometime. I have just named a beautiful Peniocereus for him which is described in the August number of the Journal of the Washington Academy of Sciences, page 328.

                    Very truly,

SMITHSONIAN INSTITUTION.
Washington, U.S.A.

ALL CORRESPONDENCE
SHOULD BE ADDRESSED
TO THE SECRETARY

UNITED STATES NATIONAL MUSEUM
INTERNATIONAL EXCHANGES
BUREAU OF AMERICAN ETHNOLOGY
NATIONAL ZOOLOGICAL PARK
ASTROPHYSICAL OBSERVATORY
INTERNATIONAL CATALOGUE OF
SCIENTIFIC LITERATURE

September 20, 1922

My dear Deane:

This letter will introduce Mr. Ivan M. Johnston who, as you doubtless know, is to spend the next year or two as an assistant at the Gray Herbarium. Mr. Johnston has done some very fine work in the Gulf of Lower California where I had collected ten years before. I have been very much pleased with his work and I believe that he has the possibility of becoming a very fine botanist. Anything that you can do for him will be very much appreciated.

Very sincerely,

J.N. Rose

Mr. Walter Deane,
    29 Brewster Street,
        Cambridge, Massachusetts.

Washington, DC

September 20, 1922

My dear Deane:

    This letter will introduce Mr. Ivan M. Johnston who, as you doubtless know, is to spend the next year or two as an assistant at the Gray Herbarium. Mr. Johnston has done some very fine work in the Gulf of Lower California where I had collected ten years before. I have been very much pleased with his work and I believe that he has the possibility of becoming a very fine botanist. Anything that you can do for him will be very much appreciated.

    Very sincerely,

    J. N. Rose.

Mr. Walter Deane,
    29 Brewster Street,
        Cambridge, Massachusetts.

My dear Deane:

Indeed I have not forgotten you. I was writing about you yesterday — but work and — see!

The "Cactus" picture you send is that of Euphorbia's splendor!

We are all well. George comes home tomorrow. We all send love

Your friend
J. Rose

I have just had a letter from Prof Coulter. He is just back from China.

THIS SIDE OF CARD IS FOR ADDRESS

Walter Deane,
29 Brewster St.,
Cambridge (38)
Mass.

SMITHSONIAN INSTITUTION
UNITED STATES NATIONAL MUSEUM
WASHINGTON, D.C.

This correspondence taken from Mr. Deane's vol. 1 of Britton & Rose, Cactaceae

April 18, 1924.

Mr. Walter Deane,
 29 Brewster Street,
  Cambridge, Massachusetts.

My dear Mr. Deane:

 Your very kind letter of April 13th came duly to hand. As I told you on my postal card, I had just been writing about you, although I did not tell for what purpose. The enclosed correspondence will explain itself.

 It is a great pleasure for me to send you a complete set of the four cactus volumes. I have long wanted to do it, but was not quite certain how the matter could be handled, as the number of personal copies which came to me at first were only a very few, and these I was obliged to dispose of in a definite way. I am especially glad that these volumes will reach you on the 23d of this month. I hope the day will be a very enjoyable one for you. Mrs. Rose and I have had the date in mind for some time, but we were somewhat surprised when you wrote us just how old you would be on that day.

 What you tell me about Ivan Johnston is very interesting. He is a very fine young man and we all think a great deal of him. I wish he were to remain permanently at the Gray Herbarium. Next to having him here in Washington, I would rather see him there than anywhere else. I did not know until your letter came that Miss Vincent had left the Gray Herbarium. I was so sorry to hear of Miss Day's death. She certainly was a very fine person to have charge of the Library. She was always so accommodating and so very helpful. I had a long and interesting correspondence with her.

 You will be interested to know that George came home yesterday for a week's stay with us. He is getting along fine in his work. He is looking forward to going back to Harvard next year, and in case he does I have no doubt that you will see a great deal of him.

      Yours very truly,

      J. N. Rose
      Associate Curator,
      Division of Plants.

(Enclosure)

April 14, 1924.

Mr. Walter Gilbert,
　Carnegie Institution of Washington,
　　Washington, D. C.

My dear Mr. Gilbert:

　　Mr. Walter Dean, 29 Brewster Street, Cambridge, Massachusetts, is an old and valued correspondent and friend of mine. In fact he is a friend of every botanist who has visited Cambridge since the days of Asa Gray, of whom also he was a friend. He has often helped me in getting information from the Gray Herbarium when I needed it, and, although he has not aided us very much in the Cactus investigation, I still feel that he ought to have a set of the Cactus books. Under the circumstances, however, I think that this had better be charged to my personal allotment. If this meets with your approval, will you be good enough to have the four volumes sent to him at the above address so that they will reach him not later than April 23d?

　　　　　　　　　　Yours very truly,

　　　　　　　　　　J. N. Rose
　　　　　　　　　　Associate Curator,
　　　　　　　　　　　Division of Plants.

CARNEGIE INSTITUTION OF WASHINGTON
WASHINGTON, D.C.

April 15, 1924

Dr. J. N. Rose
   United States National Museum
      Washington, D. C.

My dear Dr. Rose

      In reply to your letter of yesterday we shall be glad to send a set of the Cactus monograph to Mr. Walter Deane, 29 Brewster Street, Cambridge, Massachusetts.

      These books will be charged, as you suggest, to your personal allotment as co-author.

                Very truly yours

                Administrative Secretary

CARNEGIE INSTITUTION OF WASHINGTON
WASHINGTON, D.C.

April 15, 1924

Mr. Walter Deane
    29 Brewster Street
        Cambridge, Massachusetts

My dear Mr. Deane

At the request of Dr. J. N. Rose we take pleasure in sending to you, under separate cover, a set of the Cactus monograph, Publication No. 248 of the Carnegie Institution of Washington. We trust that you will accept these volumes with the compliments of the author and of the Institution.

Very truly yours

Administrative Secretary

SMITHSONIAN INSTITUTION
UNITED STATES NATIONAL MUSEUM
WASHINGTON, D. C.

May 2, 1924.

Mr. Walter Deane
29 Brewster Street,
Cambridge, Massachusetts.

My dear Mr. Deane,

    Your cactus specimens came to hand yesterday. I think my guess sent on a postal card was about correct, that is, your plant is probably Nopalxochia phyllanthoides, a very common plant in cultivation and also a great favorite. Whether it is exactly the same as the wild form or not, I am not quite sure, in fact, I don't believe that I have ever seen the wild plant. It has been in cultivation for hundreds of years and has doubtless been changed more or less. It has ~~usually~~ passed as a specimen of Epiphyllum, but you will note that it has not the long slender tube which is characteristic of that genus. I have had your specimen dried and will preserve it in the Cactus Collection. You will find a little more about it in my last Cactus volume.

                Very truly yours,

                Associate Curator
                Division of Plants.

SMITHSONIAN INSTITUTION
UNITED STATES NATIONAL MUSEUM
WASHINGTON, D. C.

October 6, 1924.

Mr. Walter Deane,
  29 Brewster Street,
    Cambridge, Massachusetts.

My dear Mr. Deane:

Various letters have been received from you from time to time, none of which I seem to have answered. I am writing now, however, for a special purpose; that is, I want to extend a very cordial invitation for you to come down to Washington during the latter part of December, spend Christmas with us, and stay over for the meetings of the American Association for the Advancement of Science. Mrs. Rose and the girls are all very anxious for you to come. George will be home from law school, and we trust that we can make you have a very delightful time. Please let us know at once that we may expect you.

I have been having some very nice letters from L. H. Bailey and he has been sending me some very fine specimens collected by him in northern and central Brazil. He has written me once or twice about the serious illness of Mrs. Bailey. I suppose he has written to you about the same matter, but in case he has not, you may be interested in his letter of October 2d which I am enclosing for you to see. I thought that in case you had not heard from him you might like to write to him.

I am also enclosing a copy of Berger's review of my cactus book and also a personal comment which appeared in the Wabash Record.

I suppose Ivan Johnston is again back in Cambridge. I must write to him in a few days.

Yours very truly,

J. N. Rose
  Associate Curator,
    Division of Plants.

(Enclosures)

SMITHSONIAN INSTITUTION
UNITED STATES NATIONAL MUSEUM
WASHINGTON, D. C.

(Rec'd
Jan 19

January 16, 1925.

Mr. Walter Deane,
   29 Brewster Street,
      Cambridge, Massachusetts.

My dear Mr. Deane:

    Your card of January 12th came duly to hand, but your box of cactus specimens mentioned therein did not reach me until yesterday. These I have identified as follows. The little slender specimen is undoubtedly a seedling of <u>Opuntia versicolor</u>. It ought to have small leaves subtending the spine clusters. I think I can observe the small leaf scars in your specimens. The round specimen with hooked spine is what has long passed as <u>Mammillaria grahami</u>, but you will find it treated in the fourth volume of my cactus monograph as <u>Neomammillaria microcarpa</u>. Figure 174 resembles very much your specimen. The original plant was collected by Emory about 1848, and was described by Doctor Engelmann, I believe, from his notes. A few years ago I had one of my collectors go back to the very spot where Emory collected his plant and send me some specimens which proved to be the same as <u>Mammillaria grahami</u> of our collections.

                           Yours very truly,

                           J. N. Rose
                           Associate Curator,
                              Division of Plants.

SMITHSONIAN INSTITUTION
UNITED STATES NATIONAL MUSEUM
WASHINGTON, D. C.

May 12, 1925.

Mr. Walter Deane,
   29 Brewster Street,
      Cambridge, Massachusetts.

My dear Mr. Deane:

    Your letter of May 9th is just at hand. I am glad to learn that the photographs reached you in good condition. The orchid photograph is the one of the Holy Ghost plant about which Mrs. Rose wrote you some time ago. I suppose you observed the dove in the center of the flower. By the way, Mrs. Rose wished me to ask whether you had received her letter or not.

    I intended to enclose with the photographs a copy of the description of Roseocactus which appeared in February last, and consequently you were not able to find the name in the cactus book. This simply goes to show how unstable or perhaps incomplete our botanical knowledge is of any of the great groups of plants. Since the appearance of the monograph three new generic names of cacti have been dedicated to me; Roseocactus, Berger, of which you have the photographs; the genus Roseia by A. V. Fric of Prague; and Brittonrosea by Spegazzini of Argentina. It seems to me that I am getting more than my share of generic names.

    Mrs. Rose and I have just received an invitation to the unveiling of Doctor Gray's bust at the Hall of Fame of New York University next week. We should both love to go, but doubt whether we can or not. I suppose I owe my invitation to Doctor Robinson who, I see, is to deliver the address. I have also been invited to attend commencement out at Wabash College this year and I rather expect now that I shall go out for a few days.

                   Yours very truly,

                   J. N. Rose
                   Associate Curator,
                       Division of Plants.

COPY   Wabash College,
             Crawfordsville, Ind.
             April 27, 1926.

Dr. Joseph N. Rose,
Smithsonian Institution,
Washington, D. C.

Dear Doctor Rose:

    Wabash college will confer upon you the honorary degree of LL.D. in case you present yourself at the college gymnasium at ten o'clock Saturday, June 13th. We feel that we shall be more highly honored than you if you consent to accept this degree. What is your reaction in the matter?

    With very kind regards to you and Mrs. Rose, I am as ever

    Sincerely yours,

    /s/ G. L. Mackintosh.

SMITHSONIAN LOCAL NOTES

Issued Every Other Week for the Information of the Employees of the Smithsonian Institution and Its Branches

Friday, June 19, 1925.

Secretary and Mrs. Walcott left Washington Saturday, June 13, for the usual season of geological field-work in the Canadian Rocky Mountains. They will assemble their outfit at Lake Louise for the start into the mountains. They expect to return to Washington the latter part of September.

The following solar-constant results refer to the first decade of June:

June	Number of Values	Mean
1-10	10	1.919

NATIONAL MUSEUM
NATURAL HISTORY BUILDING.

Dr. Waldo L. Schmitt, Curator of Marine Invertebrates, is spending the month of June at the Tortugas, Florida, where he is making a study of the Crustacea of the region under the excellent facilities provided by the marine biological laboratory of the Carnegie Institution.

Mrs. Agnes Chase, assistant agrostologist in the Grass Herbarium, has returned from Brazil with her collections.

Professor A. S. Hitchcock is attending an alumni meeting of the Iowa State College at Ames.

Dr. J. N. Rose received an honorary LL.D. degree from Wabash College at Crawfordsville, Indiana, Saturday, June 13.

Mr. B. H. Swales has recently presented to the U. S. National Museum six birds from Madagascar and five species new to the Division of Birds.

Dr. Peter Suschkin, the eminent Russian ornithologist who has been studying at the U. S. National Museum for the past month, left June 3 for a tour of the West with Mrs. Suschkin before returning to Russia. He expects to stop at the Museum early in August for a week before finally sailing for home.

Dr. Bartsch has given a number of talks since the last issue of these Notes. On June 4 he addressed the Scientific Club of the Public Health Service on "The hobbies of a naturalist." On June 5, at the inter-city Scout Meet held at Bolling Field, he gave a talk to about 600 Scouts from ten of our largest eastern cities, on "The advantages of the scout camps to the scouts," stressing the nature study program. On June 13 Dr. Bartsch conducted the camp fire activities of the local Boy Scouts at Camp Woodrow Wilson, Burnt Mills, Maryland. It will be remembered that the 48 acres of ground constituting this camp were given to the local council of the Boy Scouts of America by one of our regents, Mr. Brookings. A large turn-out was present at Saturday's meeting, which marked the opening of the Camp for the summer season. On Tuesday evening, June 16, he addressed the Arts Club on "Birds and men—a comparative study of animal behavior."

Doctor J. W. Gidley of the Division of Vertebrate Paleontology is leaving for Florida to work in cooperation with the Amherst Museum expedition led by Professor F. B. Loomis in a further investigation of the Pleistocene deposits of that State. He will leave here next Sunday and expects to be absent from the Museum for about 2 or 3 months.

Doctor August F. Foerste, specialist in Paleozoic paleontology, is spending the summer at the Museum to forward his studies of the Museum's collections of cephalopods and cystids, a work upon which he has been engaged every summer for several years past.

MEETINGS IN AUDITORIUM AND ROOMS.

June 29-30—Auditorium and Room 43—Federal Horticultural Board—Public hearings on the subject of fruit and rose stocks and the white pine blister rust—9 A. M. to 4:30 P. M.

ARTS AND INDUSTRIES DEPARTMENT.

An interesting exhibit in the Division of Graphic Arts consists of the Lord's Prayer, engraved by Mr. Alfred McEwen, shown inside of the eye of a sewing needle, magnified 145 diameters. About 13,500 complete prayers of 56 words each could be engraved in one square inch, but this is very large compared to one of these micro-engravings measured by the Bureau of Standards, which is so small that it took 781,050 to cover one square inch. This is equivalent to 43,694,000 words. The micro-engraving on exhibition in the Smithsonian, made February 10, 1925, is very clear and distinct. It was engraved on glass, with a diamond point, by means of a pantograph. The machine itself is as wonderful as the work it does. The first machine to do work of this character was invented and used by the London banker, W. Peters, in 1852. Fifty and sixty years ago, micro-engravings were quite common, but at present are very rare.

In times of war, microscopic messages could be sent engraved on the edge of a shoe nail, on a ring, a brass button, an eyeglass, or any object that is smooth and hard, and these messages would be practically impossible to locate except by the one who knew where to look.

Dr. John Uri Lloyd of Cincinnati, Ohio, recently contributed, for addition to the historical collections of the Division of Medicine, an old surgical instrument which was in vogue when the operation of bloodletting was more popular than it is now-a-days. This instrument, which is known as a scarificator, consists of ten blades set upon two rotary axes and operated by a strong spring. The blades being set the instrument is placed upon the skin and the spring released, whereby ten shallow incisions are made. An "exhausted cup" (one in which the contained air has been rarified by the combustion of a small quantity of alcohol) being applied a continuous flow of blood may be maintained until the desired amount is withdrawn. This instrument and an early type ophthalmoscope are the latest donations of Dr. Lloyd, who has rendered very valuable cooperation for several years in developing the historical medicine, surgery and pharmaceutical collections.

A recent visitor to the Division of Mineral and Mechanical Technology was Mr. Henry A. Bomberger, of Philadelphia, who is preparing a lecture on the history of aeronautics. He was particularly interested in the aeronautical models which have been made by the Division and also commented upon the many historical aircraft exhibited. With the assistance of the section of photography he was supplied with photographs of the aeronautical collections and given data which will be incorporated in his forthcoming lecture.

In LOCAL NOTES for June 5 it was announced that the Assistant Curator of the Section of Wood Technology had begun a series of talks to ten classes from the Science Department of the District of Columbia Public Schools under the direction of Mrs. M. S. Gillson, General

asic Limestone Conglomerate Metamorphosed by Intrusive Diabase at Leesburg, Virginia," by Earl V. Shannon.

Proceedings Separate No. 2571, entitled "A Further and Detailed Description of the Type of Elephas roosevelti Hay and Descriptions of Three Referral Specimens," by Oliver P. Hay.

Proceedings Separate No. 2574, entitled "Notes on the Meteoric Stone of Colby, Wisconsin," by George P. Merrill.

Proceedings Separate No. 2575, entitled "Studies on the Larvae of Crabs of the Family Xanthidae," by O. W. Hyman.

Proceedings Separate No. 2577, entitled "The Genus Pentacrinus in Alaska," by Frank Springer.

Proceedings Separate No. 2578, entitled "A New Meteoric Stone from Baldwyn, Mississippi," by George P. Merrill.

Proceedings Separate No. 2580, entitled "A Revision of the Parasitic Wasps of the Genus Microbracon occurring in America North of Mexico," by C. F. W. Muesebeck.

Proceedings Separate No. 2585, entitled "Revision of Bugs of the Family Cryptostemmatidae in the Collection of the United States National Museum," by W. L. McAtee and J. R. Malloch.

Proceedings Separate No. 2586, entitled "A Review of the Beetle Family Pneudomorphidae, and a Suggestion for a Rearrangement of the Adephaga, with Descriptions of a New Genus and New Species," by Howard Notman.

Proceedings Separate No. 2587, entitled "The Dragon God (Dai-Ja) in Idzumo, Japan (a Japanese Tale)," by I. M. Casanowicz.

Proceedings Separate No. 2589, entitled "Two New Larval Nematodes belonging to the Genus Porrocaecum from Mammals of the Order Insectivora," by Benjamin Schwartz.

Title Page, Table of Contents, and List of Illustrations to Proceedings, Volume 64.

Proceedings Volume 64.

LIBRARY ACCESSIONS.

MUSEUM.

Adam, Leonhard. Buddhastatuen.
Britten, F. J. Old clocks and watches and their makers.
Gisecke, Walther. Sicilia numismatica.
The librarian guide; general catalogue of Polish books.
New York. Metropolitan museum of art. The restoration of ancient bronzes and other alloys.
Newstead, R. Guide to the study of tsetse-flies.
Werner, A. G. New theory of the formation of veins.
White, R. Senior. Catalogue of Indian insects. Pt. 3-4.

LIBRARY OF CONGRESS.

Ashton, T. S. Iron and steel in the industrial revolution.
Frobenius, Leo. Erlebte erdteile.

OFFICE.

Levitt, E. H. The rigid airship.

BUREAU OF AMERICAN ETHNOLOGY.

Fox, C. E. The threshold of the Pacific.
Frobenius, L., and Obermaier, H. Hádschra Máktuba Urzeitliche Felsbilder Kleinafrikas.
De Labriolle, P. History and Literature of Christianity.
Parker, F. H. A Thousand Years of the Tartars.
Perrier, E. The Earth before History.
Sonntag, C. F. The Morphology and Evolution of the Apes and Man.

Wabash College
Crawfordsville, Indiana
June 22, 1925

Dear Dr. Rose:

Though I had no memorandum of my remarks at the granting of your degree, I can recall practically all, as follows:

"Dr. Rose, I also had the pleasure of welcoming you, years ago, to Wabash College. However, as I was then a Sophomore and you a Freshman the welcome may have lacked the desirable quality of cordiality. Not so today, but far otherwise. Your achievements in the science of Botany are known not only in America but to botanists the world over. We are proud of you. In comparison, I am, I feel, scarcely worthy to be the medium through which this degree is conferred upon you. Here at Wabash, we are honored by your presence and acceptance of this degree. By virtue of the authority vested in me by the Board of Trustees of Wabash College, I confer upon you the Honorary Degree of Doctor of Laws."

Sincerely yours,

G. L. Mackintosh

SMITHSONIAN INSTITUTION
UNITED STATES NATIONAL MUSEUM
WASHINGTON, D. C.

February 5, 1926.

Mr. Walter Deane,
   29 Brewster Street,
      Cambridge, Massachusetts.

My dear Mr. Deane:

    Thank you very much for your kind letter of recent date. You will be interested to learn that I have just had a letter from the manager of the Huntington Estate, asking me to submit an estimate of the probable expense of the investigation I mentioned in my recent letter. Later on I hope to send you a copy of this correspondence.

    If you have not already disposed of the editorial which I sent you, will you be good enough to return it, as I may wish to send it on with my estimates? If you have already disposed of it, no harm is done as I think I can arrange to get another copy.

                  Yours very truly,

                  J. N. Rose
                  Associate Curator,
                    Division of Plants.

rec'd Dec. 13/26

Smithsonian Institution,
Washington, D. C.,
December 9, 1926.

Mr. Walter Deane,
   29 Brewster Street,
      Cambridge, Massachusetts.

My dear Deane;

    I have been wanting to write to you for a long time, but have been so busy and have had so little help since I finished my cactus work that I have neglected every thing except strictly official matters. I am writing now to say that I will probably be in Boston for a day or two next week, appearing there as a Government witness. I am to tell the August Court why a "prickly pear" is not a "pear." From this you see that the study of cacti has a practical side to it! I hope to spend atleast one evening with you. I shall telephone you as soon as I get located in Boston.

    Hoping to see you soon,
        I am your friend,
           Sincerely,,

SMITHSONIAN INSTITUTION
UNITED STATES NATIONAL MUSEUM
WASHINGTON, D. C.

January 29, 1927.

Mr. Walter Deane,
   29 Brewster Street,
      Cambridge, Massachusetts.

My dear Deane:

    I left the Gray Herbarium last Friday afternoon about 4 o'clock. I tried to get you on the phone, but was unsuccessful. I reached Washington Saturday morning, being delayed nearly an hour on account of the terrible fog in and about New York City. I suppose you noticed from the papers that all outgoing ships were much delayed that day.

    I had a most delightful visit in Cambridge and accomplished a great deal of work. I was especially glad to have had several nice talks with you, and I want to thank you again for your kindness to me. Please remember me to Miss Brown.

    I think I told you that we won our case. I have just had a very nice letter from the Railroad Administration about it, a copy of which I am enclosing.

    With regard to your picture with the hummingbird: I want to say that you gave one of these to George which he prizes very much indeed. We do not have the picture of Mrs. Deane, but Mrs. Rose says she will be very glad indeed to have it if you have a duplicate which you can spare. I have been terribly busy since my return home, but hope to have more time later on when I will try to write you again.

    Some of our Washington men have re-discovered a very rare <u>Chelone</u>, and I find that Doctor Pennell of Philadelphia has a good specimen. I at once thought that you ought to have this in your herbarium. If you want it, write to Doctor Pennell yourself. I am enclosing his letter.

                         Yours very truly,

                          J. N Rose
                          Associate Curator,
                            Division of Plants.

(Enclosure)

COPY

Washington January 24, 1927.
File 585-2279-C

Director General (Erie Railroad) vs A Aloisi & CO.

Dr. J. N. Rose,
Associate Curator,
Division of Plants,
Smithsonian Institution,
U. S National Museum,
Washington, D. C.

My dear Dr. Rose:

    I beg to acknowledge receipt of your letter 22nd inst. in regard to above case and have just been advised by the Boston attorneys that the trial resulted in a judgment for plaintiff. We are very much indebted to you for your assistance in the matter and am sure that the verdict was due largely to your convincing testimony. I have conferred with Mr. Andrews who has very kindly agreed to approve a voucher for your expenses and same will be forwarded to you in the next few days.

                Very truly yours,

                    /s/ H. D. Boynton
                        Attorney

HDB:R

THE ACADEMY OF NATURAL SCIENCES
OF PHILADELPHIA

DEPARTMENT OF BOTANY
FRANCIS W. PENNELL
CURATOR

LOGAN SQUARE
PHILADELPHIA, PA.

January 27
1 9 2 7

Dr. J. N. Rose,
   Division of Plants,
      United States National Museum,
         Washington, D. C.

Dear Dr. Rose:

        I have reviewed the two descriptions that you sent and am enclosing these. It is a pleasure to feel that certain groups of my Colombian Collections are receiving such careful study.

        Yes, I have a number of duplicates of <u>Chelone obliqua</u>, and can send one to your correspondent as desired. I am glad that you are finding so much of interest in the specimens loaned from our Herbarium.

        Sincerely yours,

        Francis W. Pennell
        Curator of Plants

FWP:S

SMITHSONIAN INSTITUTION
UNITED STATES NATIONAL MUSEUM
WASHINGTON, D. C.

April 9, 1927.

Mr. Walter Deane,
    29 Brewster Street,
        Cambridge, Massachusetts.

My dear Mr. Deane:

Your letter of April 6, with my copy of the evidence taken at the pricklypear trial, has come to hand.

With regard to the word "pricklypear" written as a solid word: I wish to say that it is so used in "Standardized Plant Names," a catalogue of approved scientific and common names of plants in the American Commerce, based on Bailey's Cyclopedia of Horticulture, published in 1923, and prepared by Olmstead, Coville and Kelsey. I am quite aware that the name is used differently in most botanical publications, like those enumerated by you, but for my purpose it seemed well to quote the latest authorities on this subject, especially as it made my case stronger. Page 17 was omitted because it applied to something not related to my testimony.

I have just had a charming 4-page letter from the Judge who presided at this trial, among which things he says, "your whole scientific evidence was not only interesting, but convincing, as the jury's finding showed."

Some time ago Doctor Bailey sent me a very interesting memorandum regarding herbaria, some points of which I want to quote to you: "We are making good progress in botanical science and yet there are certain important phases in which we are greatly deficient and to which the imagination of botanists themselves has not been sufficiently directed. We have as yet no beginning of records to enable us to study mutations in epochs of one hundred years, and where are these records to be preserved? Some of these will be kept in universities but we need a national depository for valuable, special, and amateur collections. Certain of such collections on which critical monographs are founded, or that represent particular regions or botanical groups should be preserved intact by themselves. Contact should be kept with growing conditions to the end that those with no direct or natural designation may eventually be gathered as parts of the National archives. I know of the great value of the collections there (in the National Herbarium) and of the excellent contributions that are making by competent and devoted workers. Some parts of the collections are outstanding in the world,

Mr. Walter Deane-2.

as the grasses, Cacti, ferns, and others. We need more material, more perfectly prepared, and a higher herbarium technique with greater accessibility to the public. All these ends should be attained in a great country like this with its wealth of material and resources, and I think that all will come when the subject is forcibly presented to the people."

I wrote to Mr. Coville under date of March 3, commenting upon Doctor Bailey's letter, among which things I said: "The new balcony that is to give additional room for the herbarium will be sufficient to take care of the normal growth of the herbarium for the next ten or fifteen years. At the end of that time the question of housing the collection will again be acute. I can well understand, however, that if the National Herbarium should receive the proper support that it deserves either through Government funds or private donations, that it may before the end of that period need additional room. The logical handling of this would be for a new botany building for the Government. Just where this should be located is a minor matter. It has been suggested that such a building might be put up in connection with the new arboretum, while as you know, a prominent man of Congress who has been greatly interested in the Arboretum (Mr. Luce), has suggested a location on the south side of the Mall."

If we succeed in developing our collections as we have planned we shall eventually have a magnificent botanical department.

Yours very truly,

J. N. Rose
Associate Curator,
Division of Plants.

Smithsonian Institution
U.S. National Museum
March 7, 1922 — Washington D.C.

My dear Doctor Bailey:

Thank you very much for your letter of March 4. After spending eight days at John Hopkins University Hospital, and having been looked over by Doctor Longcope and Doctor Barker, two of their ablest men, I am back home again and, at their suggestion, have taken up my work once more. They found no organic trouble of any kind, so there seems to be no real reason for me to be sick. I think I am getting a little stronger day by day although the change is rather slight.

Yours very truly,
J.N. Rose
Associate Curator
Division of Plants

EDITORIAL OFFICE
ITHACA, N Y

L. H. BAILEY

This is good news from Rose.

I got home on time It was good to have seen you again.

Ever thine

L.H.B.

L.H.B. to W.D.
mar. /28

SMITHSONIAN INSTITUTION

UNITED STATES NATIONAL MUSEUM

WASHINGTON, D. C.

March 17, 1928.

Mr. Walter Deane,
  29 Brewster Street,
    Cambridge, Massachusetts.

My dear Mr. Deane:

    It is very good of Doctor Bailey to turn over my last letter to you. I have been intending ever since I got back from the hospital three weeks ago to write you, but have neglected it from time to time.

    Mrs. Rose would have written, but she has had her hands more than full. Early in the week she was obliged to go to the occulist's herself to have her eyes treated. George has been out of office several days with a bad case of sinus trouble and was obliged to go to the doctor's twice a day. He is better now and goes only once a day, and is back at office. Rebecca has had serious trouble with her antrum and has been away from the office several days. Yesterday they took her to the hospital to be operated upon, and she is now in the Episcopal Eye, Ear and Throat Hospital under the care of two doctors. My mother, who has been with us all winter, was taken dangerously ill last Tuesday and has been confined to her room, under the care of two nurses ever since, with a temperature up to 103 a good part of the time. She still is very sick and is not yet out of danger.

    You see we have had plenty of things to keep us busy at home. I am some better myself and am at the office each day, but am taking things rather easy.

    I hope you are feeling better yourself.

                           Yours very truly,

                                J. N. Rose

SMITHSONIAN INSTITUTION
UNITED STATES NATIONAL MUSEUM
WASHINGTON, D. C.

April 7, 1928.

Mr. Walter Deane.
29 Brewster Street,
   Cambridge, Massachusetts.

Rec'd Apr. 10
Ans'd

My dear Mr. Deane:

Your card has just been received this morning, for which we wish to thank you. I have been intending to write to you for some time, but we have had so much on hand that I have put it off from day to day.

George is much better, and is back at his office again, but goes to see an expert every day. Rebecca has been home for some time, but has been gradually growing worse. She is to be operated upon again today at 12:30. They are to pull one of her upper teeth and through this opening are to get into the sinus. It appears to me that it is a very delicate and trying operation. I do not know how long she will be in the hospital this time, but possibly two weeks or more.

On March 13 my mother, who has been spending the winter with us, was taken desperately sick and soon developed pneumonia which took her away on the 23d. I went out to Indiana for the funeral, coming back the following Monday. I have not felt quite as well since my return as I did, but hope to be feeling better again shortly.

I had a very enjoyable call from Dr. L. H. Bailey yesterday. He went down to Tennessee to deliver a lecture and stopped in a few hours on his way home.

I trust you are feeling quite well.

Yours very truly,

J. N. Rose
Associate Curator,
Division of Plants.

WESTERN UNION

CLASS OF SERVICE

This is a full-rate Telegram or Cablegram unless its deferred character is indicated by a suitable sign above or preceding the address.

SIGNS
DL = Day Letter
NM = Night Message
NL = Night Letter
LCO = Deferred Cable
CLT = Cable Letter
WLT = Week-End Letter

NEWCOMB CARLTON, PRESIDENT   J. C. WILLEVER, FIRST VICE-PRESIDENT

The filing time as shown in the date line on full-rate telegrams and day letters, and the time of receipt at destination as shown on all messages, is STANDARD TIME.

Received at

10FY G 41 NL

WASHINGTON DC A-PRIL 22

WALTER DE˙NE

29 BREWSTER PL

DOCTOR AND MRS ROSE AND THEIR CHILDREN JOSEPH REBECCA MARTHA AND GEORGE AND THEIR GRANDCHILDREN JOSEPH DOROTHY GEORGE AND WALTER DEANE ROSE SECOND WANT TO CONGRATULATION ON REACHING YOUR EIGHTIETH BIRTHDAY OUR LO.E AND BEST WISHES GO WITH THIS MESSAGE

NO SIG
8.26A

every day.
We are having most delightful weather. Rebecca has been carrying a sprig of spring to her teacher for the last week. This morning she took a crocus and a dandelion.

Mr. Rose and I hope we may see you and Mrs. Deane in Washington before very long. It is too bad to have the boy grow out of babyhood without your seeing him.
We both send a great deal of love to you and Mrs. Deane.
            Sincerely,
Mch. 18th '98   Mrs. Simes Rose

My dear Mr. Deane:

Yesterday afternoon the expressman brought a very interesting looking package to our door and asked if "W. L. Rose lived here" — the girl said "no," but upon seeing the address on the box said, "Oh yes, Walter Deane Rose lives here."
Upon opening the box we found the beautiful

arrived. How I wished
Walter Deane might enjoy
the opening of the package.
Indeed we must thank you
and Mrs Deane both for
the beautiful gift to our
dear little baby.
I think Mrs. Deane could
not have chosen a more
artistic and appropriate
design.
We are so glad that your
name is on it — as years
to come this will add to the
interest and value of the
dish to our boy.
We can fancy how if our

[left page, sideways:]
dreams of being the father of our boy's life, in years
to come the many lessons we have learned
and other Walter Deane's may use it
in these tiny hands.
And the dear little letter of yours Walter
Deane will prepare his mother for, indeed
it becomes him — it will be carefully put
away for him.
I do hope you might see him with your own and
say he is a splendid boy & he is as little
... we hope become — from the agreement ...

[illegible]

[illegible] them [illegible]

[illegible] of the [illegible]

Sincerely,

[illegible] Rose.

Aug 2 '78.

Washington, D.C.

[illegible]

I do not think that

Rose [illegible] half enough

[illegible] been [illegible]

[illegible]

[illegible] hear [illegible]

[illegible] explain

[illegible] he [illegible]

[illegible]

laughs [illegible]

I think he has the [illegible]

sweetest smile [illegible]

[illegible]

"He has two to
for all they los
hence they are - ;
from the neural
of ta tion and
teeth at once
This is enough
up of his super
I am quite as

My dear Mr. & Mrs. Horne

I wish to tell you how sweet we thought the pretty Christmas greetings, and above all the thought and affection that inspired them.

I shall put Walter's name away with his little letter, so that he may have it when he is older.

The young gentleman is at this moment on the

My dear Mr. Hearn:

Baby Walter Hearn desires me to acknowledge your very kind letter. I wish so much you might see him. He is so large and strong and sweet — such an affectionate little boy and so fond of his papa. He has the whooping cough but is almost [well]. Has not had it very [bad]. So he has been

allowed to a few bread crumbs — but he is not starved.

I hope you are not tired of hearing so much about Walter Hearn. His father is thinking seriously of Mexico again. I dread to think of his going so far away and yet I cannot bear to have him keep him at home if he thinks it necessary to his work.

We both send love to Mrs. Hearn — Sincerely,
Lou Hi

February 26. 1899.

it required rather delicate handling to balance the blocks. I thought that quite good for so small a boy. He is trying to walk alone and when he does take a few steps, smiles in a very self-satisfied way —
He knows each member of the family by name but all he attempts to say is "ah!" I hope he is to use his lovely tongue just as soon as he begins to take solid food.
Now he takes his bath without linens and cuffs from a bottle — and

...use for weeks.
He is so tall now that he can stand at the window and look out and when he sees his papa coming he begins to shout and pound on the the window pane with his little hand. He is also quite a builder. I watched him at play the other day — He had his blocks — among them were some ten pins — he stood a ten pin on the floor then placed two other blocks on top of the ten pin — the head of the t.p. being quite small

My dear Mr. Dean:

Your kind letter was forwarded to me here. I was surprised to learn that Mr. Rose had not more fully informed you of his plans — but you must forgive him as he was so very much pressed for time up to the last hour of his stay in W. Indeed he remarked two or three times before he left that if he did not get away soon he was afraid he would break down.

Well — he brought me here to his mother's and stayed a day with us. He left on last

[May 4]
Thursday, going back to Cincinnati and then down by way of New Orleans then on to El Paso — stopping over for a day at Houston.
I had a letter from him at Houston — he had a lovely day there — found the Principal of the High School to be a warm friend of Mr. Pieters of W— and also of Mr. Hicks. This gentleman and three of the high school teachers devoted themselves to him during the day — he collected a good many plants in the afternoon. He expected to reach El Paso on Monday afternoon, where he was to meet

his assistant Mr. Hemphill—
No he is not going to undertake such a trip as he did before— he intends keeping close to the railroads and depending on the good hotels rather than the natives for food. I would have been very unwilling to have him go as he did before — for he was sick with malaria nearly all of the next year. His next address will be Buena Vista Hotel — City of Mexico. He expects to be there in ten days or two weeks— He will meet Mr. Pringle there — which will add much to his pleasure.

trip very well — he was frightened at the tunnels but slept like an angel all night.
He is already his grand mother's delight — and tyrannizes over her like a king.
His delight is to go out on the asphalt walks and pull leaves as he passes the flowers. He is also much in love with the chickens and horses.
I have been missing Joseph and Rebecca through the mumps since I came.
Please give my love to Mrs. Keane and forgive this long letter — but I knew you wished to know a little of Mr. Rose's Klaus.

I am glad you were pleased with the pictures — They are not as clear as we desired but are very like our dear little boy.

    With kind regards —
      Lon Sims Rose.

Liberty
  Indiana.
May. 11 — '99.

My dear Mr. Deane:

A letter from Mr. Rose yesterday brings one enclosed for you. He is still sending Joseph stamps. This accounts for the roundabout journey your letter has taken.

We are all pretty well — though little Walter Deane has not been quite as well as I could wish — but still he has done remarkably well for a teething baby — He now has sixteen teeth.

Will you forgive my maternal weakness when I tell you he is the very dearest baby I

Raymond I am quite sure that you and Mrs. Deane would think so too.
You should see him as he goes out on the walks with his chubby hands behind his back. There is a long cement walk out to the gate and it is his delight to go back and forth over this walk — stopping to look at the flowers — but he never breaks one — his grandma thinks this is wonderfully good for so young a child.
We had a very happy fourth. The children and I — we were up bright and early firing fire crackers — Then a walk to the woods — In the evening

fire works and company –
We always give the day entirely
to the children –
I am hoping Mr. Rose will
be with us before many weeks.
He said in his last letter
he hoped to reach El Paso not
later than Aug. 1.
We are counting the days until
he returns –
    Give my love to Mrs. Lheam
and I know if Walter Lheam
was awake he would send his
love to you –
        Sincerely,
          Sm. S. Rose –
        [Mrs. J. N. Rose]

July. 2. '99.

My dear Mr. Deane:

As Mr. Rose is very very busy just at this time I think I will not wait any longer for him to write for Walter Deane but do so myself.

Yesterday afternoon a large strong box came to our door. Of course the children wished to open it at once but I suggested we wait until their papa came home since we always share happy surprises.

When Mr. Rose came of course the first thing was to open the box. Then Walter Deane lifted the inside lid and I wish you could have heard his delighted little chuckle. Then the fire engine was lifted out and while it was being adjusted he laughed and laughed. He seemed to understand at once that it was his own.

Then you would have thought there was a "really truly" fire, could you have heard the noise and shouts and seen those fat little legs running up and down the house.

It is too bad that you have [illegible] more seeing her pleased [illegible] [illegible] you [illegible] [illegible] good [illegible] [illegible], [illegible] in a very [illegible] little boy [illegible] [illegible]. he would [illegible] you [illegible] [illegible] [illegible]

The children are all [illegible] well now. Martha is still [illegible] so slight [illegible] [illegible] has a good [illegible] [illegible] [illegible] [illegible] [illegible] [illegible] a few weeks she [illegible] her old self.

[illegible] [illegible] when she came home and they [illegible] [illegible] well. [illegible] [illegible] hospital

and Martha and [illegible] [illegible] are the [illegible] all the [illegible] [illegible] [illegible] [illegible] small [illegible] [illegible] [illegible].

Please [illegible] [illegible] [illegible] [illegible]

Sincerely
[illegible]

Feb. 13. 1900

My dear Mrs Deane:

Mrs Rose begs me to tell you something more of Walter Deane. I cannot tell you a single wonderful thing that he has done, nothing but that he is a normal happy baby for 27 months. He eats heartily and grows peacefully for his tender years & sleeps "like a little kitten" and when he is awake He is all smiles and fun just as noisy as he can be. He dearly loves a doll and must have "Doll" as he says, in his little bed where he takes his naps and when we press to bed at night.
I took him yesterday to see a little neighbor— the baby sons of Mr. O. F. Cook they have two very animated parrots one an African and one from Porto Rico. Walter Deane was de-

lighted and at once tried to whistle as they did.
We have lately sold one dozen chickens to our possessions and Walter Deane is never so happy as when he is leaning against the fence watching them.
He is trying now to talk but he seems a little slow about it.
I wish you and Mrs. Deane could just have one of his bear like hugs. He is so affectionate.
When Martha gets hurt he runs to her and puts his arms around her to comfort her.
Now you must be tired — this is not very interesting to any one but Mr. Rose and me.
But I must say that Walter Deane is, whether it is the result of his name or being his father's son — he is the dearest baby in all the world.
   Sincerely
   Mrs. ...... Ina S. Rose.

[Washington, D.C.
Aug 11 1912]

Dear Mr. & Mrs. Deane:

I hope you do not think I am forgetting my dear dear Deane for one moment, but the last week has been almost too much for me. Mr. Rose leaving was almost more than I could bear — It seemed as if I could not endure the terrible separation at this time — and then before he had reached New York came the awful news — so I have just been stunned —

It is a heart breaking task for me — because I am reminded on every hand of the dear loving boy.

Of course I have given away everything that would be useful to any boy — as I think it is wrong and foolish to keep things — But there is so much else.

The pictures are wonderful. What a good camera yours is. 841 — is a picture of Rock Creek near the new ford. The Sherman statue is just South of the Treasury.

I could not write — I did not dare to think. Sunday we all went to church — and after dinner went out to Chevy Chase to see some dear friends — I felt that we could not stay at home. Sun make before service our dearly beloved one sat at the round table — Sunday only four.

I am so sorry Mrs. Dean has been ill — did she over do here — or what was it. Oh how I wish you were both here. I think we almost need you too — you dear, dear people.

This is the day of the regimental drill of the High School Cadets. The President will review the drill. These drills make the boys very tired. They sometimes faint. I am hoping that our soldier boy will get through all right.

Mrs. Lee gives a musical this afternoon — I hope we can go but I am not sure. Yesterday we cleaned closets six of them — and Emma is doing three more —

I am so very glad to have
the pictures — yes I will be
very glad to send the film
that we talked of.
I will send it by registered
mail — as it will be safe.
You have certainly had a
busy week — but now you
must rest and have a good
vacation.
I do hope Mrs. Sheane is quite
herself again
We still talk over your visit
and both of you — you do not
know how much we all love

you — from dear people —
and I pray we may
all be spared to have
another good visit here
next year — only a longer
one.
With dearest dearest love
for you and dear Mrs. Keane
Ever lovingly
Sue Annie Rose.

Martha will be shocked if she
sees I have turned my
paper upside down!!

Dear Mr. Deane:

Kept to our own pain our hearts turn to you.

I want to tell you that our beautiful darling — we know that his body so beautiful and unblemished was only a likeness of his soul. We know he was clean and pure and belonged to Christ.

But oh how can we bear

to do without him.
Every one loved him as and
sometime I want you to see
some of the beautiful messages that have come to
us.
I can not write more now
I wish you and Mrs. Deane
could be with us.
With love to you both
Mr Lumm Rose

My dear brother,

as by we could fix. Even winds Sunday night
—, a cousin who visiting & Tomcas and her reaching
[illegible]. We had to so our little cora school is always
of noise — [illegible] dismissed at 2 o'clock. but
to her Say, our family owing to the storm the children
to so to Hellen Keane, were sent home with me —
It might re[illegible] — The accident occurred jus[t]

[illegible] rather [illegible]
have [illegible]
[illegible]

[illegible]

[illegible]
to me [illegible]
[illegible]
[illegible]
[illegible].

[illegible] Thursday
the chapel of [illegible]
[illegible] assistant -

made a most beautiful
prayer [illegible] carried [illegible]
[illegible] away.
The [illegible] School [illegible]
acted in full [illegible]
and [illegible] embarrassed [illegible]
[illegible] school came in
full uniform.
[illegible] [illegible] minister whom
we really love and admire
made a [illegible] and
told what kind of a [illegible]

"Gran Hotel Maury"

VISCONTI Y VELÁSQUEZ – SUCESORES
de ANGELO BERTOLOTTO

Casilla Correo No. 1103
TELÉFONOS:
Nº 133 Y 1652
Cable: LOTTO
Lima – Perú
RESTAURANT DEL PARQUE
Zoológico y Botánico
TELÉFONO 515

Rec'd July 29/1914

Lima, July 12th de 1914.

My dear Mr & Mrs Deane:

Your good letter came this evening and I assure you it was most welcome – being the third letter we have received since we left U.S. Mr. Rose is busy all the time with his collected plants. But he said he would write you soon.

We arrived in Lima two weeks ago today on the Peruvian Steamer Pachitea and had a very delightful voyage. The west coast was a continuation of sand dunes – no vegetation – We stopped first at Payta – a town of about 10.000 – We anchored in the harbor and went ashore in great flat row boats. It was quite thrilling going down the side of the boat and the ride across the Bay most beautiful – I have a picture of the boat and oarsmen. The town and surrounding hills were absolutely devoid of one sign of green – The town was very unclean – This is where the Panama hats can best be bought. The Indians bring them to the ship – and they are very fine hats and very reasonable. Our next stop was made at Pacasmayo – where we again went ashore – This town was clean, well paved and nice looking

people. Mrs. Rose went to the hills and I stayed with a party of young people – we went to the R.R. Station – and suddenly out of a door came two of the dearest little girls – pretty and neat. They then came right up to us and curtsied so nicely and shook hands – Then came an Indian maid with white cap & apron and a darling baby and after her the mother – She seemed so glad to see us and nothing would do but we must go into her parlor – We told her our names and she wanted us to have tea – Then she wanted the young people to dance the tango – So one of them played on the piano and they danced for her and sang. Then she sent for her husband who proved to be the Superintendant of the R. R. Then she wanted to take us to a friend's house who has a very large and fine collection of Inca relics and a beautiful butterfly collection. So we all went there. Senor Montenegro. He had such a pretty wife and sweet daughter and nice home.
He sold his first Inca collection to some one in

Lima. de 191

England. They wanted to see some one dance
the Turkey trot - Hesitation and the Tango.
Doesn't it seem odd.
So again the young folks danced and sang,
their pantom spread out on the sea and it
was beautiful - I commenced to worry about
Mr. Rose for I had promised to meet him at the
end of the pier which is very very long.
But it was quite dark then. Senor Conway-The
R.R. Supt. ordered out an engine and coach
to take us to the end of the pier.
When we stepped outside of the house
I met Mr. Rose with the trainmen hunting
for me - so he met them and we all
rode over together. But they were such charming hospitable people. The next stop was
made at Salaverry where we met the U.S.
consul. Large shipments of rice and sugar
are made at Salaverry and oranges
and rice at Pacasmayo.
We are here at this quaint hotel - we are very
comfortable and the hotel people are very kind
in deed. We have a suite - a sitting room
opening on the interior court - a bed room and
back of that a balcony with windows - It seems

has ever shone in our rooms. We have a man who takes care of our rooms and waits on us. The office closes at ten o'clock. The lights are out and the place is very quiet for about two hours. Mr. Rose p brought an electric stove with which to dry his plants and we find it a great comfort — for it is very cold and damp here. There is no heat in the building and no way of heating it. The sun seldom shines here and much of the time a fine mist is falling — too as we came over trillac — The streets are very wet — sloppy and oh so dirty.

The town is not pretty — The buildings are not kept clean and in repair. They seem to have excellent street car system — and their great heavy carriages drawn by two horses and as the streets are paved with small cobble stones — you can imagine the noise. The women here all seem to wear black — The Cholo women or servant class wear a soft black shawl draped over the shoulders and head — ladies wear the very black lace

Lima, dec 19¹

mantillas. The shops are poor and second class and pawn shops everywhere. It is there tourists go to pick up souvenirs. I saw a mummy's arm in one for sale as well as lovely carved fans and tortoise shell combs.

We have been over to Chosica — up in the foothills where the sun always shines — it is a sort of winter resort for Lima people. It is about 25 miles from Lima and on the celebrated Oroya railway — There is a very good hotel there — Then last Wednesday we went still further up the same road to Matecuana — It is 1000 ft above the sea — such a wonderful climate — not so the hotels fortunately I could have soft boiled eggs and tea. Mr. Rose found 12 different cactuses there besides other things. We saw such lovely heliotrope there — it seems to be native to the spot — bushes as tall as I am and such lovely fragrant flowers — and sweet violets — The railroad follows the Rimac river the valley is very narrow and this is said to be one of the most wonderful R.R. feats in the world — The R.R. reaches the highest altitude in the world. Saturday we were invited to luncheon at the home of Mr. Markle. Mr. Rose knew Mr. Markle and Mrs. Markle in Mexico years ago. He is was President of The Ferro Carill Central of Peru. Mrs. Markle is ill in Canada – So he is all alone with the servants. He lives at Miraflores – a half hour's ride from Lima and a most beautiful spot. The house is one story surrounded by a lovely garden and all enclosed with a wall 8 ft. high – The home is perfectly beautiful inside. He is greatly interested in rare old furniture and clocks – He has five grandfather clocks – Think of it – when most of us would be delighted with one – He has a tortoise shell and ivory cabinet in the drawing room – he says there is one other like it in a Museum in Paris. In the hall is a wonderfully carved hall seat – I suspected it was a part of an old choir stall – he said yes – it came from an old church in Mexico. But the inlaid tables and chests and urns – and wonderful carved leather chests and such wonderful colors – Then he opened a chest in the hall and took out three gorgeous embroidered shawls – one in white one in pink and one in rose.

"Gran Hotel Maury"
Casilla Correo N°. 1104
TELÉFONOS:
N° 133 y 1652
Cable: LOTTO
Lima — Perú
RESTAURANT DEL PARQUE
Zoológico y Botánico
TELÉFONO 515

VISCONTI Y VELÁSQUEZ — SUCESORES
de ANGELO BERTOLOTTO

Lima, ... de 191..

Then he opened a cabinet containing the old Spanish silver stirrups and spurs and aprons and tools. Well it was a rare treat — and he so charming and delightful, and yet a great R. R. and mining man — we have been told he is the most powerful man in all Peru — and yet when we went to the English, American Episcopal church this morning — he was the first person we saw — he introduced us to the Rector — and Mr. Sharples read all the Scripture selections during the service. He is evidently the strong man in the church as well as every place else. It is against the law here for the Protestant Church to have a church edifice here — so they built this church to look like a Spanish dwelling outside but a church inside. A bill has been introduced in the Senate asking for religious liberty here.

I must tell you that in Mr. Markle's drawing room the floor was covered with a lovely rose colored rug — and in the very center was a snow white alapaca rug. The effect was beautiful.

We have had a real earth quake. Mr. Rose and I were both in the hotel and we heard the unusual noise and not until I heard the beams and rafters twisting and creaking did I realize the cause.

No plaster is used here — the ceilings are just plain wood.

Then on Sat. morning about five oclock we were awakened by such a terrible noise in the street I was sure the revolution was on hand again — I ran to the balcony window and it looked like all Lima was on fire. The fire was in the next square and the fire engines were so little we felt afraid they could do no good — So we got up and dressed and prepared to leave in case of necessity. But by six — the people came back and went to bed again — So you see we have had some excitement. There was a Bull fight here this P.M. — every one went — but us — I do not care for such things — We went out to Mucon — a sea side resort and saw the strange water birds feeding on the beach.

Mr. Rose goes to Aroya tomorrow to be gone several days — I had intended going too — but Mr. Markle thought I might have "siroche" which might in

"Gran Hotel Maury"
VISCONTI Y VELÁSQUEZ — SUCESORES
de ANGELO BERTOLOTTO

Lima, _____ de 191_

very bad for my heart — he thought I would be very unwise to go.

I wish you could see our sitting room. Mr. Rose has two corners filled with cactuses. One corner with the electric stove and a package of plants hanging over it — The other corner has driers, baskets and a press — yet we have a parlor set, a pier glass and a center table.!! Oh yes and the base of the pier glass is covered with jars of formaldehyde containing cactus fruits — I cannot say it looks like home — it looks like some one was busy.

I do hope you can write to the girls — you do not know how far away they seem and they think so much of you. I miss my boy here more than ever & and I fear my courage is failing for it seems as if I must have him.

I have written a very long letter — tell dear Mrs. Dean not to think of writing — not to visit any yet sleep for I do want you to visit us next winter in Washington — I will write often and do keep well. We will be here until the last of July then we will go to Arequipa for a month and then to Santiago. You might send a line to Arequipa care of Prof. Campbell and to Santiago care of

Oddo Hotel.

Mr. Rose joins me in love to you both. I hope you will not be vexed after reading this volume — but I thought you might like to know what we had been doing.

Sincerely
Mr Hume Rose.

Arequipa Peru.
August 30th 1914.

My dear Mr. & Mrs. Deane:

Your dear letters came this morning. I cannot tell you how welcome they were for my heart has been so heavy with our terrible sorrow. and to have your dear letter this morning and to know that you understood so well what we have lost and how we feel – so it is not necessary to say they were more than welcome – and I do appreciate dear Mrs Deane's writing – but she must not do any thing to strain her eyes but must just get well and strong for you must come to M— during

I was not well and Mr. Rose felt that our surroundings were rather impossible so the next morning he went to see a Mrs. Bates – of whom we had heard from other friends – She is an American woman who has lived here for over 30 years – a really gifted woman – one who has seen all sides of S.A. life and who herself has known many hardships – and yet with it all has kept a certain sweetness and kindliness that you must love and admire. She has the nicest home here – a large house standing in the midst of a lovely tropical garden and she fills her house with people who come to her recommended by some one she knows. She at once agreed to take us and even gave up her own room to do so.

the winter and make us a visit. As the time draws near for the opening of the schools. I think of our dear boy's hope to go away to a Preparatory school. He was so ambitious and wanted so much to be a good man — oh do you know he is ever with me. I feel that I must reach out and take him in my arms — I was so proud of him even vain that he was mine. We were always as sure of his truth and fidelity to duty — I am not forgetful of my other precious ones — but will life ever be right without him.

Forgive me for this giving way — you don't know how much I am with the struggle to be brave.

We have stayed in Ste Guipa much longer than we ever dreamed of. We arrived here the evening of July 30th and went at once to the Grand Central Annex Hotel. It is in a small building — new and clean with rooms. The rooms were tiny boxes containing two beds a wash stand and a set of stuffed furniture — not a wardrobe, drawer or even a nail in the wall. They seem to think a set of stuffed furniture is all that one can ever desire in the way of comfort. We went for our meals to the main hotel. A good country farm milk, horses cows etc. would have been a palace compared to it and yet we had roast chicken soup and a baked apple for dessert. It seemed so odd to see a real friendly, homelike, baked apple.

but I know if I were ill it would worry Mr. Rose and hinder his work. Arequipa is 7800 ft high and the atmosphere is so wonderfully clear – the days are very warm and the nights very cold – so cold we have to put on heavy dresses for dinner. We are just at the foot of Misti which is most beautiful – and when we go up on top of the house – we see not only snow capped Misti but into other snow covered ranges. It is interesting to watch the snow some mornings we can see that more snow has fallen in the night – and just in Mrs. Bates' garden calla lilies are in full bloom – the loveliest poppies and snap dragons – for just a minute I saw a peach and pear trees in full bloom

The house consists of ten rooms besides the dining room and kitchen a wonderful balcony and a side porch where afternoon tea is served. Our room is very large and looks out on a small street. We have one very large window and that has heavy iron bars all over it and outside of the windows are planted very thorny cacti – all of the windows are barred in this way. I'm sure you would be surprised at the dainty appointments of our room – it seems marvellous that a woman who lived 20 years in a mining camp and so many years has a similar room here to live there

things — and in this room we have real feather bed now. You will smile at this — but not since we left Colon have we had feather pillows — they are stuffed with wool and are hard as wood. We have electric lights and a nice bath.

We have an odd mixture in the way of travelers. Mr & Mrs Green — English — he is 73 — she 42. He is a mining engineer and she is always talking about American husbands "I'm poor they are etc !! He is very English and patronizes the American — says he has never read Lincoln's Gettysburg speech — though he understands it is a very clever speech! Have a friend with them a Miss Ford — she says "igNore"

all the time and we suspect she is very proud of each one.
Miss Liralle a small Spanish girl.
Miss Buco a German — who is an oculist's assistant and a fine woman.
Mr. Basadre a Bolivian gentleman — very refined and very kind — he told me his nephew graduated at the Univ. of Illinois last Spring and has gone to Berkeley to take an engineering course. So you see we represent many different countries.

Mr. Rose left this morning for Cuzco where he will meet Dr Eaton of the Yale exploration staff.

I have not been able to go any higher than Arequipa because of my heart. Mr. Rose spent two weeks in La Paz. I was greatly disappointed not to see La Paz and Lake Titicaca.

There are beautiful cases of shining instruments & sterilizer & baby incubator — but alas the doctors do not know how to use them or what they are for! They have no nurses and no money. The nuns nurse through the day and at night the Chola women take charge. The chola women are the native servants and would not be allowed in one of our hospitals until they were fumigated. In each ward there is an altar — and the poor sick women looked so odd — all wrapped up in ugly tt brown shawls. The Madre Superior is French and rich — The government allows the poor sick 14 centavos a day for food which equals 7 cents of our money.

scarlet geraniums. One peach tree is filled with bloom and has a half ripe peach on it and there is a lemon tree in the garden that Mrs Bates depends on for her lemons. The oranges here are most delicious sweet and juicy and the figs are ripe.
Mr. Rose and I have been to the market which is really a beautiful building and very interesting. It is not considered the proper thing for ladies to go to market here nor do ladies or gentlemen carry parcels. One must have a barefooted Indian - dirty and ragged & carry all packages even a pound of candy

I must not forget to tell you the names of the servants here in the house. They have many in each household — about seven here besides the gardener. Marie is the cook. She is a fierce looking Indian woman — and rules the house. She has a little servant to help her — a chubby face boy who washes the cooking utensils and who loves to say "Buenos dias senora" to me when he gets a chance. Fortunatus — Scholastica and Ascension — They are all named for a saint.

Housekeeping of the right sort is carried on under many difficulties. The servants are lazy — even filthy and dishonest — Water is scarce and fuel is scarcer still. They cook with a dried corn tillifer. It is light and burns easily but smokes so dreadfully — we are taking some home to show you —

The sewers are all open and we would become sceptical as to the danger of germs could you see the people drinking this water — washing in it and using it in every way. It is most horrible. We drink a mineral water called Jesus water — pronounced Há sus —

Last Sunday I went with Mrs Baker to visit the Sn gripa hospital. The hospital was given to the city by a very rich man. It is the most beautiful hospital I have ever seen.

The operating rooms are dazzling in their whiteness and nickel fittin

...e, rais[e] with her own money bought cattle, sheep and chickens so as to provide milk and eggs for these poor people. I thought this a beautiful charity.

This is a Catholic stronghold and the priests are very corrupt – consequently the people have no morals. Legal marriages are rare and you are depressed by the hopeless condition of the people.

Financial conditions are very bad. It is impossible to get money and all business is very very dull. One cannot but wonder what there is in store for this [poor] country. These people are simply ignorant children

In consequence of our prolonged stay here we have not heard from the children as I fancy their letters have all gone to Valparaiso.

We hope to leave here next week if we can get a suitable steamer.

I hope I have not gone too much into detail.

If Mr. Rose was with me he would I am sure join me in sincere love and best wishes for you both. You are both very dear to us and if my letters do give any pleasure or interest then I am happy in this.

May God bless you and keep you and give you health and strength —

Sincerely
Ann Sine Rose

Interior del Hospital Goyeneche, Arequipa.

Comunicaciones

Tarjeta Postal
(Solo para la Direccion)

Rio Chile, Arequipa.

Tarjeta Postal
(Solo para la Direccion)

This shows the river Chile in the foreground. Hardly a river — but very important here. Mista at the back.

rec'd Aug 7 1914

Lima.
July. 12 – 1914.

Dear Mr. Deane:

We got three postals for you last evening – Mr. Rose wanted to write you but he is so rushed, so I offered to send you a line & guess it will not be nearly as interesting but you will understand.

We returned last night from Iroya – to reach this point which lies between the two great ranges of the Andes – we had to pass over the western range at 15,645 ft – The postals are pictures of two of the bridges on this wonderful R.R. In about 50 miles there are 60 tunnels – This is the center of the llayama industry and he says

the mountains were covered with tree strange animals.

He says the flora was very interesting, a slight attack of soroche left him with very little strength and not much enthusiasm for collecting.

He made this trip especially to study that strange cactus described by John Ball in his Notes of a Naturalist in S. A. page 92.

You should see our sitting room and our balcony — Two corners of the sitting room are full of cacti — in the other is the electric stove with the press hanging over it. In the fourth corner are baskets, dryers etc. — In the

In the pier glass are jars of quartz and flowers and one S. A. mouse. This is not my ideal of a lady's parlor — but science must be encouraged.

Our love to you Wittie.
We expect to leave here July 28th on the Pachitea — for Mollendo — from there we go directly to Arequipa. Here we will very likely be through August.

Sincerely
Mr. Lina Rose.

Rec'd Oct 30 /14

Santiago
Chile, October 3rd 1914

My dear Mr. & Mrs. Deane:

We arrived in Valparaiso three weeks ago to-day. We left Arequipa on the morning of Sept. 7, going to Mollendo by rail and there taking the English S.S. Ortega. When we left A. the sun was shining as it always does there but when we reached M— it was dark and foggy and cold.

We were delighted with Valparaiso. It is almost entirely a new city and very modern and substantial. It has very large German & English colonies. The city is almost entirely built on hills that rise from the Bay — and each hill or precipice has one or two ascensors — so high and steep are the hills. The bay is beautiful and at night one can see the entire city and the thousands of electric lights like an [fairy?] city from the hills. We met some very pleasant [people?] there — Dr. John Sommerville

The hotel at Mollendo is almost beat description – Boiled eggs and boiling water was all one felt would be safe from the "hand of man". The water there is nearly always rough and on that day said to be the worst in 30 yrs. When we started to go aboard we could not go down the steps to the small boat – but were seated in a special chair then swung out over the water by a special iron crane and let down into the boat. I thought I could not endure that terrible swinging out into space – but Mr. Rose stood on the back of my chair & we went down together – The ride across the bay to the steamer was thrilling – we were sometimes up and sometimes down – But when we reached the ladder at the steamer's side then came the test of nerve and rapid thinking. Our little boat was rising and falling about 15 ft with every wave – to step on the wet and slippery ladder at the right moment and then to climb up the long ladder was a trying experience – I did not recover from the strain for several days.

One can always see here the snow covered mountains. The city is so clean and so well built — and the people look so superior to the Peruvians. We went to see the military review — The soldiers have the same uniform as the Germans and have German instructors. They have such fine horses. It was interesting to see the aviation corps with their flying machines — the radio telegraph corps with their equipment — The scene was one of great beauty — the bright uniforms, the gay pennants of the cavalry, the green pine trees just tipped

and Mrs G. His father was sent there over 70 years ago as a missionary and he built the first church on the west coast — the first in the continent — This son, the Dr. was educated at Yale and graduated in Mr Taft's class. He is a most delightful man and full of fire and energy. We also met and saw much of Mr Simons, a young Englishman who is manager of one of the largest Nitrate companies in

while. He was delightful and good.
We came to Santiago a week ago Thursday.
The ride between V and S is wonderfully beautiful. The yellow California poppies were in all their glory all along the R.R. The peach trees in full bloom — the hills and mountains green — the farmers plowing the fields with oxen.
We saw one hacienda entirely surrounded by a rose hedge in full bloom — great creamy roses with pink centers — it was wonder-

ful.
Then we saw so many cactuses. At one station the women had flowers to sell, enormous bouquets — for one peso — about .15 in our money. Mr. Rose bought one for me and I could scarcely carry it.
It had over 13 different kinds of flowers, calla lillies, ever so tall red + pink roses — daisies lilacs syringa — snap dragons — wisteria and many others.
Then at another station they were selling baskets of tunas custard apples — oranges and lemons.
Santiago is very lovely and very fine — it is very like Paris.

but I could not bear to see more.

We have met a Dr. & Mrs Browning – missionaries. He has charge of the Instituto Inglesa – a boys school. He has 120 boarders from all over S. A. and 120 day pupils. The Brownings are very delightful people – we heard him preach at the Union church last Sunday – and he gave a splendid talk on "My young man". Of course it made me sad for I could not think of our young man who left us just on the threshold of life's work and he was so pure and fine and splendid – I do not seem to gain strength as

the parade ground, and back of there rose the mountains entirely covered with snow. Mr. Rose has found much to interest him in the Museum. He has seen all of Phillippi's cacti. The Quinta Normal is very beautiful.

The parks here are well kept and well laid out.

Mr. Rose left this A. M. for Copiapo – on the Longitudinal road. The R. R. is all but closed on account of the financial trouble here. He will travel 3½ days, only days, to reach C. It is all desert and a very hard trip. He was not willing that I should undertake it. The Chilian Gov't. has given him passes etc. This is a delightfull hotel. Beautiful and clean and very good food. only they serve so much meat. We nearly always have five or six meat courses and no green vegetables. The Chilians are fond of meat. The women take no exercise eat a great deal and do little to cultivate their minds.

The daughters are taught music dancing and embroidery. Can you imagine a pretty girl nowadays who cannot play tennis or walk. The men — the rich men choose Law & Medicine for professions. The women are very fat and faint so much. The streets are full of automobiles and the most beautiful horses and carriages — and yet Sunday afternoon we had a trouble riot in our street. I stepped out on the balcony as the mounted soldiers came charging up the street

to me it must be very like the cities of Palestine. I wish I could picture to you the sunlight as it falls in the evening on the flat roofed pink blue and gray buildings, the church spires and domed the purple and rose shadows on the snow capped mountains. I have written a volume — do for give me — I have rather imposed on you this summer — but you are both very near and dear to us, do you think our boy knows how we love him! Mrs. Rose told me to give her love to you both when I wrote. I do hope we will be starting home before many weeks later as long as the children are not well I see the months go by but rather lose my courage — did you know of the sad sad death of his friend, Lee Wade III? There are days when I cannot believe it is true — that we laid our beautiful boy away — it seems so cruel to think we could calmly do it. Do you know that when we start from Valparaiso for home it will take us from Xmas — if we succeed in getting a steamer at once in

Colon!
I must not forget to tell you of our visit to the Observatory at Arequipa.

We went the afternoon before leaving.

We hired one of the Ford autos, another for their two mile trip. We crossed the Sampa river and then for nearly two miles drove through the old old part of the city, streets so narrow that people had to get into doorways or around the corner before we could pass. And the people and the children!! so many and so dirty — pigs babies & dogs raced ahead of the car.

I never saw so many dogs — this in the road that leads to the Observatory. The house is very nice and the grounds lovely. It is just at the foot of Mista. Mr. and Mrs. Campbell were very kind and served tea for us. Then Prof. C. took us to see the great photographic telescope. It is indeed very wonderful and very interesting. I felt so sorry for the Mrs. C. I understand they are very poor and both look very delicate. He is a hard worker.

Arequipa is the most foreign city I have ever seen — it seems

Tarjeta Postal

Washington D.C.
December 23rd, 1914.

My dear Mr & Mrs. Deane:

It is dreadful, I think, [that] we should [have] let time or two slip by without sending [you] a line, but I think his picture never stepped into such a perplexing medley of interests and amusing matters as we did when we arrived at our home the night [...]

But we took the little bride right into our hearts and home for she is a dear, dear girl. I did wish a little for her sake as well as ours that we could have had some warning— She came to us [...] joining her father in [...] judge of the circuit court and her uncle is in congress.
It was not a runaway match, they simply had a quiet wedding at the bride's home. They stayed over Sunday and went back on Monday for Joe could not be away long.
I [have found] a young lady

... ...
que to have out under the
... ...
well we can imagine we evening
so much to talk about.
The ride told us time of the
marriage the day before.
~~Saturday~~
Please do forgive this delay
for I intended this as a Christmas letter. On Saturday morn
while we were at breakfast Joe
and his bride arrived.
Of course we were terribly surprised

to see ... ...
picture of ... darling George
... was so close
and had had a long
discussion on the journey
as to who was to meet us
at the station — so you can
imagine our anxiety — knowing the girl's devotion — I felt
alarmed — George finally
admitted that Rebecca had
been ill — When we reached

Mr. Rose had feared it was lost or missed — He left last night at midnight for N.Y. — Rebecca says that all we'd do any more is to say Good Bye to each other. So you see why letters are not written to the dear dear friends our hearts yearn for.

We had our Christmas tree in the Library and the same friends took dinner — my old teacher Miss Crawford, a friendly bachelor brother Mr. Haskell — Mr. Rose's cousin Judge Jones and from Concepcion & the States a Miss Medina. She came to study Art. She is a Chilian and speaks beautiful English. She is very intelligent and very ambitious. She was educated in the M.E. college at Concepcion although her father & mother are Catholics. The father became dissatisfied with the mission schools and mailed his daughter to have something better — Well she came & was with us and was here for ten days. While she was a dear lovely girl yet she was a responsibility and I had to help her get some clothing etc.

She is now in Pasadena with a friend studying Painting and Vocal Music. Before she left Mr. Rose was called to Indiana to attend to some business for his mother and he was kept there two weeks.

Before he returned Rebecca's friend Miss Clotilde Grunsky stopped here for a visit on her way home to San Francisco. She is a dear girl and her coming was such a joy to Rebecca — They were devoted school friends.

I should have mentioned that when she came Martha came home from Baltimore quite ill with cold — so I put her to bed and called the Dr. and she remained in bed a week — Last Tuesday my cousin and dear friend Mrs. Vanderbilt came to spend Christmas with us — The day before Christmas Mr. Rose had a telegram from N.Y. telling him that his collection from southern Peru, shipped for N.Y. on September 7th had just arrived and was in excellent condition —

Mr. Rose will stop in
Philadelphia with Dr. B—
for the A.A.A.S. meeting.
I hope you will forgive our
delay and remember we
think of you and we all
send much love and
wishes for a Happy New Year.
  Ever Sincerely
   Jno S. Rose

my cousin — from lonely
people — We had a simple
dinner — The same lovely
and ever more tonight to
our — friends came in
in the afternoon and eve-
ning and yet he whom
we loved so dearly I sometimes fear I am slipping
him, never came ..
I saw him just as he was
a year ago with his dear
smile and beautiful eyes
yet I lived through the
day and hid my grief.

Your dear card came — and comforted me — But I have not found peace. It is just as far as ever from me, — I cannot give him up.

George is six ft. tall and so like Walter Deane in so many ways — in fact he seems to grow more and more like him. He is a dear boy. Dear Mr. and Mrs. Deane we are so anxious to see you — could you not come and make us a visit very soon — any time would be convenient for us — we have a sunny spare room and a bath next to it and a good red cork and I am sure we could make you very comfortable. We do long to see you and talk to you and I think it would do Mrs. Deane good — now do consider this. If you can come right away we will be so very glad.

Washington D.C.
February 21st, 1915.

My dear Mr. & Mrs Deane:

It is a long time since I wrote to you — if thoughts were letters you would have been flooded.

Your dear telegram on our boy's birthday came and it was dear of you to remember us — The hardest and most painful day I have passed since he left us.

He used to take such joy in the

Mr. Rose is planning to go to S.A. again. The girls and I will probably go to some quiet spot in New England, while we hope to send George again to Culver — He needs the physical training — he was so debilitated last summer —

And now I must tell you the object of this letter —

We are counting much on your coming to see us this Spring — and we do not want you to fail —

Now what do you think of coming in April. The weather is mild here and Washington is

day - We always made so much of the day - I can see him as he sat at the table on his father's left with his dear sweet smile as he opened his packages - Then he would get up and kiss each one of us.

On my last birthday he gave me an electric drop light - He was so dear to me - No wonder that the very sunshine is dark to me - when I know he is not in it.

We went for a walk across the hills this afternoon - a walk he so often took with us - a place he played in when a little boy.

George has grown so tall and is so like him in manner and voice.

He is a very good student and shows some evidence of writing well - His ballad is to be published in the "Westerner". We will send one to you. His table is filled with things rather unusual for a boy of 14 - He has read much as to the cause of the present war -

beautiful in the Spring.
Do not let the Spring pass
without coming. I feel as
though life is getting more
and more uncertain for
all of us, and we must
meet again in this world.
I would give much if we
had the memory of your
seeing Walter Deane.
He talked of it constantly
and looked forward to
seeing you — and used to
ask me if I thought you
would like him

what a young man he would be today if he was here. For you know I can not always believe he is not here.

So dear dear Mr and Mrs Sloane do come to us this Spring — We will take good care of you. Our house is large and comfortable. You can rest and do just the things you desire — and if you eat special things we will have them for you. So talk it over and let us know when you can come. The entire family send love and earnest invitation for your visit —

Your sincere friend
Mrs Susan Rose

Washington D.C.
March 19th 90

My dear Mr & Mrs Arscome

I am sending just a
line to tell you how glad we
are that you are really
coming on the 9th April.
We are looking forward
to seeing you with much pleasure.
The joy however be in your
visit will be saddened by
the absence of the dear dear

we do want this visit to be
a rest and pleasure to you
both — our home is quiet and
I think you will not have
to change my great —
With love and best wishes
and the precious hope of
seeing you soon — Be sure
and let us know the hour
and road that we will
take I am sincerely
M. Louise Rose

just as you please.
Indeed we will meet
you at the station and
we can drive in the
car to the station which
and come to me now
[illegible] a new book [illegible]
[illegible] take our beautiful
[illegible] continue.
[illegible] remark-
ably sunny — but [illegible]
[illegible]

me — who so longed to see you.
There was much we long
to talk over with you —
for you held a relation to
dear [illegible] because that
no one else did.
Now Mrs. [Lecane?] must not
write a word — and do not
feel that there will be any
strain in your coming —
just come as if you were
coming to another home

Washington D.C.
April 5th 1915.

My dear Mr. & Mrs. Deane:
Just a line to tell you we are counting the days until Friday.
The weather is mild and Spring like now — though Saturday we had a great storm. Snow and wind all day. Easter was beautiful.

We will meet you Friday night — think of it — this week. I can scarcely believe it — it is too good —
I pray you may come in all safety.
We all send love.
Most Sincerely
Sr Anna Rose

You would have been interested to see the great crowds of children black and white, young & [older], [...] and [...] [...] with Easter eggs. [...] [...] was closed to all vehicles today so that children might play in [...] at safety. wasn't that lovely?
Mr Rose leaves tonight for New York for several days — He will be at work with Dr. Britton

Lonely Washington –
April 28th, 1915.

Dear Mr & Mrs Keane:

Your letter has just come on the afternoon mail – a postal this A.M. and one yesterday – for all of which we are most grateful.

You cannot imagine how large our house has suddenly grown – There seem to be no one in it. No gentle mur—

The lame man said "Please thank Bruno for me."
We still talk of "the great surprise" – and Mr. Mahan said the whole thing was lovely – Mr. Hanna [&] says you are a pair of dears. –
These are only a few of the comments we hear on all sides from those who met you.
I can assure you your visit was no greater and sweeter joy to you than it was to us, and I can truthfully say

ments in the guest chamber
overhead - no one in
the library - and the table
seems so lonely - it seems
impossible that the long
anticipated visit has
really taken place -
I am going to comfort my
self by anticipating another.
So please be tracing your
steps for another visit ...
it.
We have had two days of
exhausting heat today.

...
We are so sorry about the
tickets - We thought everything
was arranged - so that you
need have no anxiety in
New York - and you might
have missed [...]
It only shows that mistakes
are forever being made.
and try as we will, we can
not reach out and prevent
them
Ida says that "Mr. and Mrs.
Deane are the nicest people
she ever met and [...]

dear sweet Juette — who took
such an interest in every
thing pertaining to us and
our household as you too.
George has come from school
and is reading in the
Library with a pitcher of
lemonade at his side.
Mr. Vose is growing quite
gloomy over his approach-
ing departure — while I do
not dare to think of it —
I am happy though that the

Kronprinz Wilhelm Law
introduced and there is nothing
_____ from Chara _____.
I am enclosing some
pictures for you to keep.
I think they are good – especially
the one of you and Mr. Rose.
I presume you are dining
tonight with the Le Tut—
I hope you will have a beautiful evening.
I wish I could peep in on
Mrs. Deane and Miss Brown.

This is a stupid letter
but what can one expect
from a stupid person.
We all send our dearest
love to you both and a hug
and kiss
I hope you are rested now.
Lovingly
  Mr Ainm & Rose.

My neighbor is using her
telephone – I may have and
_____ her experience!

and we did a little shopping — Then I spent a part of the P.M. marking Mr. Rose's clothing. Then he and I went out to the silent city where my darling was laid — I took the lovely pink tude that we had before — I cannot believe it is I — who is standing by that narrow bed — surely my beloved did not leave me. The spirea and white rhododendrons were in flower. The birds were singing and everything in nature was so wonder-

My dear dear Mrs. Pearce:
What a dear woman you are. How did you do it all so quickly — a week ago yesterday you left us — yesterday afternoon a big box came to me — and when I opened it the dearest cups I ever saw. How sweet and pretty they are — They surely are like you, dear heart, dainty and lovely — You can

I express what is in my heart by saying "Thank you." My heart is full—and will we think of our loving Margaret Sleane when we use them? Oh yes dear mamma we will think of her every time but we will think of her daily all the time she is a real presence in our home... Tonight when I was wiping the dishes for Ida I thought of the dear little person who put away the silver and do you know? felt as if you must come out of the dining room every moment and gather it up. This house seems full of our loved ones even though they are so far away. The cups are in perfect condition. I took them out of the packing myself. There is not one that is marred. Yes, indeed I would tell you truly.

This A.M. I went to market all alone. The flowers are so lovely now. Then I met Rebecca & M— at Boardwalk & Fellowship

ful.
Mr. Rose is about ready to leave us — I can not tell you how I feel I am broken-hearted over this parting. I wish you were near us — what a comfort you and Mr. Deane are to us — and what a joy to have you near us.

We are all so glad that Mr. Deane is so much better. Tell him he will have to come

Mr. Rose joins one in love to you both and wishes me to tell you how pleased we are with the lovely cups. They are indeed beautiful. All the Roses send dearest love to the two dear Deanes. Give my love to Miss Brown and tell her we are sorry we let you go home.
Goodnight—
Devotedly
Mrs. Lince Rose

My dear Mr. & Mrs. Keane:

Here it is Sunday morning and the letter that I hoped each day last week to write you is just starting out. However it is still early - before breakfast time - and there is always hope that one may do better.
We are having a good deal of dark damp weather and

still very cool. Though we are living in daily expectation of the arrival of summer.
I sent you a Post on Wednesday. with an account of the drill. We went on Tuesday afternoon and the day was ideal — we sat through the drill of five companies before our own company came on the field.
They were all so alike that I could not have told George if it had not been for his <u>splendid</u> long legs.

We were especially proud when Georgie's company took second prize – ordinarily one is not pleased with second prize but the boys had drilled under such great difficulties all year being scattered over the city in different buildings – that we really thought they had no chance at all. Asst. Secretary of War – Breckenridge reviewed the boys – and he added greatly to the scene with his aide in full uniform.

Mr. B. is one of the handsomest men one could see anywhere and it is said is as good as he is handsome.
I wish you could have been with us. I've met little Charlie Buchanan — you remember him — and he was such a delight.
Breakfast is over — the children off to S.S. and I must hurry and finish this before going to church.
Mr. Hannaford our pussy minister, is going to Boston tomorrow

he will be there three or four days and will stop at the Y.M.C.A in Boston
I have asked him to call on me and as he is to dine with us today he can tell you just how we are

How about S.A. steamer — I wrote you that we would sail from N.Y. May 22nd. I learned a few days ago that that sailing was cancelled and the next one will be June 12th providing it sails. I called up the P.O. Dep

and learned that a S. A.
vessel would leave Norfolk
Va. last Wednesday morning
but she was bound for southern
Brazil and I doubt if any
mail on that steamer would
reach Rio before leaving
Bahia.
I am now sending my letters
to Rio care American Consul
General —
I do not think it will do
to send mail there after June
12. I think I will send mine
on to Buenos Aires. The steam-

if possible ? Than wer.
We had a lovely afternoon with Mrs. Some, her mother and Phillip - and then had dinner with Dr. Some

They have a pretty place and a wonderful rose garden. Unfortunately we had scarcely reached the house when the rain came down in torrents - and continued until after dinner. We arrived home at 10.30. I was thankful that Mrs. Deane did not try to go out - after I took the trip. It was very tiresome and would have been too much for her.

The Lincs are dear people and I am so glad to know them — and they are such ardent admirers of both of you — Mrs. Linc says "Mrs. Deane has the gift of the understanding heart" — and so she has. You are both too dear for words and we all long to see you again — I feel sure you will come next winter. Think of those good sleepy nights — the lovely walks and everything else. By the way Mrs. Greene, we have been going to market in a "jitney" and it is great fun. The jitney starts from our door, goes down 18th St. over through S. to 17th down 17th to H - through H - to 15½ - Penn. Ave. to 19 - 19th down back to the White House and all through those Parks to 7th & the Ave.

We had a cablegram from
Mr. Rose Wed – saying he
had arrived safely at Bahia.
I cannot even guess when
we will get a li— —
I just [?] across me
Pan A.M. – when we had a
letter and how soon he would
be home — I told him he
had just arrived — up [?]
have queer ideas of distance.
We are having great Pan-
American entertainments
here now.

THIS SPACE FOR WRITING MESSAGES.

Washington.
January 11. 1925
(Rec'd Jan 13)

Dear Mr. Pearce:—

Christmas is past. The tree has been taken out. The tinsel put away. George and Joan are gone — even the candy is gone and we are settled back in to our quiet and rather lonesome...

We had a beautiful Christmas. Among our gifts was your charming book — for which we thank you.

Then came Joan on Sunday after Christmas. We enjoyed every minute he was here. He is a dear boy. So enthusiastic and full of energy.

George was so happy to have him here. We saw many old friends and met some new men at the reception at the National Gallery on Monday. The boy, to my surprise and delight, went with us.

We have had some very hard storms since they went away.

Last evening Mrs Rine and I sat here in the Library and heard all of the speeches at the banquet dinner. What a wonderful tribute was paid him. We got much pleasure out of our-
ing radio.
Do you know Mr. Spear, who was the author of the Covin-Versa ceremonial? was so suffer. That any one knows? And have you ever seen its lovely Ghost orchid?

Mr. Rine brought a blossom home from to Ot grown home the last of the week. It is beautiful. The leaf that is as real. I wish you could see it. He has had photographs taken, and perhaps he can send you one. so nice to us now—.
The entire family joins me in love — and best wishes —
Sincerely
Mrs Aimee Rose

Ack'd
Feb. 20/s

1812 CALVERT STREET
WASHINGTON, D. C.

Feb. 17. 1928.

Dear Mr. Heane:

I am sure you will be most sorry to learn that my dear husband has been in failing health all winter — He has had a number of physicians here and been subjected to many tests X-rays and so on. The Dr. here is not very encouraging and at last Mr. Rose has consented to go to Johns Hopkins Hospital in Baltimore and place himself

1812 CALVERT STREET
WASHINGTON, D. C.

under the care of Dr. Long one of the leading doctors there.

He left tonight.

It seems almost unbelievable that he who has always been so well and strong should be so ill. He has not been confined to the house but has gone to the office each day — but that has been all that he could do.

We have had a trying and anxious winter — with his illness and the care of Joe's four children.

1812 CALVERT STREET
WASHINGTON, D.C.

Jim lost a great deal of money in Florida and has turned his energies in another direction but it is slow work.

So we are trying to help as best we can by having the children here and sending them to school. They are dear children and we love them very much but they are a care.

I hope you are very well. We think of you and talk of you very often. The family joins me in love

[upside-down at top:]
Please remember me kindly to Miss Dunn. Very sincerely yours Anna Roosevelt

rec'd May 11

1812 Calvert St.
Washington D.C.
May 9. 1928.

Dear [illegible]:—
    I think we have been
here rather [illegible] these last days
[illegible]

He passed away. He was self-intoxicated in his work and was planning new things.

His limbs ran etching of the nerve that controls the muscles. It was very gradual. He was slowly losing the use of the hands. His just and Guth. For months he had only had liquid foods cream and eggs and rich stuffs and ice cream. The very best richest things tumblers of ice cream and he ate it with indeed relish

and they were at his head
and when the casket was lowered
into the grave the yellow roses
almost covered it.
Later I hope to send you a
copy of Dr. Wood's prayer
We had two hymns sung by a
young woman who has a lovely
voice. "Abide with me" and
"Lead Kindly Light."
The cemetery was beautiful —
so sunny and filled with
tall azaleas in full bloom.
Pink and white dogwood
Snowballs etc.

When I awoke on Friday
I thought he was sleeping so
I slipped out of the room —
but on my return in a few
moments I found he was gone.
The service on Monday was
beautiful. We had it here in
our home. The casket stood
in the parlour in front of the
mantel and was literally
buried in flowers.
Flowers from everywhere
your beautiful yellow roses
were the only ones of the kind

I am afraid I have written too much. but I wanted you to know as much as possible about everything. Our meeting this am I am I have afected myself — but it was because I was called away while writing.

Forgive me spoke of your career. they were to like those you sent to Herain.

The girls will miss him —
We all send our love and best wishes to you and Miss Emma.

Very Sincerely
Lou Luisa Rose.

Washington.
Jan 7. 1929.
aug 4 9-

Dear Mr. Deane:

On this anniversary of our dear Walter Deane's birth I am writing to thank you for the beautiful story of Bambi.
The little Walter Deane who will be 9- on Thursday is delighted with it.
The delicious candy was thoroughly enjoyed by all. It was a beautiful box.
I have had much in mind the birthday of our Deane when you sent him a gold piece so nicely done up in a tiny box. Some one asked him what he got for his birthday and he said "a gold penny and a cotton."
Christmas was a severe ordeal for me - but we had the dear children to help us through.
We have had a holiday visit from "influenza"- Five of us in bed at one time!
I am the last to get up- indeed I have only been up a couple of hours- and not down stairs.

I hope you will escape it.
I thought I was immune
but I must have been too
tired to resist it.
The children and grand
children join me in best New
Year wishes to you —
I must tell you before I say
Goodnight how very much the
little grandchildren have enjoyed
the copy of Grimms Fairy Tales you
sent to Walter Deane years ago.
George 6 and Walter Deane 9
listen by the hour to the stories.
It is a beautiful copy.

Please remember me to
Miss Brown —
　　Sincerely
　　　Mrs Deane Rose.

Dear namesake.

I got a your loving letter Thursday Evening mama red it and gave a smile. I will fanke you very much for the spoon and will give you a large kiss. This is the mark that baby made. I am going to bed and

Your loving
Walter deane Rose
~~Dan~~ Joan 5,98.

Written by his broth
Joseph Rose

CUPID'S TELEGRAM

Mr. Walter L Deane
9 Brewster St
Cambridge
Mass.

CUPID'S TELEGRAM

There is absolutely no doubt whatever about the accuracy of this telegram, but should the recipient wish to have it repeated, this can be done verbally by appointment.

HANDED IN AT Quiver Square 9 AM **RECEIVED AT** PM

To My Valentine

If my love you don't spurn
please send by return a wire just to say
that I'm yours from to-day

I want to thank
you for those
presents which you
gave me and I have
enjoyed them very
much. I have been
writing poems. It is
snowing this morn-
ing. After that

190

on Christmas and
my birthday I had a
birthday party. I thank
very much for the Ch
mas gift and the five d
good [illegible] got a [illegible]
[illegible]
two [illegible] money
think [illegible]

an-   ti-
  ?   ing

Washington
October 2? 1907

Dear? G...   Dear Madame
Manny George and   We have moved to 1813
I went to see Pen   Calved at N.N. P...
on last Tuesday   come and see us
night. It was   Ou... house has 3 floors
... you ought   12 rooms 3 bath...
to...   a fine basement
...   Grandma is with us
Please write so...   now we are ju...
Good ...   the Street from t...
Your loving ...   Zoo. and when you

comed will take you to see the diferent animals especialy the birds. There is a g... near us and the b... and dare build... those in a t... and if you wil... ... School ... four weeks ago.

I am in the fourth grade now. How are you and Mrs. Deane? Papa and Grandma went to Jamestown and came ... last night. Are ... going or have

Jan. 5, 1912.

Dear Mr. Deane:

I received your letter yesterday evening and was very glad that you liked my stool. It was the one which I made last year in carpenter shop. Papa and I looked at the catalogue this afternoon but I do not quite know what I shall take. On the map which you sent I found the place where you live.
I just finished reading St. Ives and I enjoyed it very much. I have read Treasure Island

I am 5 feet 11 inches tall.
    Walter Lleane Rose

In the course of the examination for entrance there are quite a few books to be read. I have read over half of them. I hope that you decide to come on for inauguration so as to see me in the parade.

We have two drill days a week and we are getting along unusualy well on account of it being inauguration years.

I hope that you and Mrs. Lleane are well.
    From your namesake
    Walter Lleane Rose

October 20, 1912
Washington

Culver

Dear Mr. Deane.

I know that you are disgusted with me but while I was at Culver it was all I could do to even write home once a weekend since I have been home. have been so busy getting started in [school] that it has been simply impossible for me to write to you. I will first tell you why I did not send the stool I was so busy getting ready to go to Culver that [I]

would you ask them to send me the literature of the courses studied I would have to have to enter, [if I] want to come. I wish you and Mrs. Deane would come to Washington to see us I am so anxious to see you.

I will close now,
From your namesake,
Walter Deane Poe.

Lee Wade II of Harvard College take Martha to the final Ball which lasted from 9 P.M. till 2 a.m.

I asked Lee Wade to look you up but I have not had time to write and ask him whether he c'd

His address is as follows:
Lee Wade II
23 Westmorly Court
Cambridge, M.

In the first Latin Examination we had I made 97.5.

I am still anxious to come to Harvard.

entirely about it. Until the day I left so we took it to the station with us and there we found it had to be crated and ever since I have come home I have not found time to —

I will now tell you about Culver. I joined the Summer Cavalry school in which I learned to ride horse-back quite well. At the end of the term we went for a ride of over one hundred and — miles.

The last three days of school the two girls, mother, George and Cousin Alice came up to Culver. I had one of Cavalry boys.

Jan. 1, 1913.

Dear Mr. Deane:

I am writing to thank you for the splendid book that you sent me. I hope that you and Mrs. Deane had a fine Christmas.

Some of the presents which I received were: a fountain pen, four books, a box of paper, eight handkerchiefs, a box of candy and a tie rack.

Last night I stayed up til twelve o'clock to see the old year die. It was very interesting to hear all the whistles blowing and bells ringing also several boys in the neighborhood shooting off their shotguns and pistols. I went out and blew two horns at the same time making a good deal of noise.

I hope that you will come to the inauguration of the next president elect of the United States. I will march in the parade. The reason for this is I have joined the High School Cadets and they always march in the parade.

The only reports that we have received since school started have each given me Excellent in Latin. You see that I still am anxious to enter Harvard in 1916.

George and I went to the woods after a Christmas tree and we obtained a fine one.

From your namesake,
Walter Vanefisse.

January 12, 1913

Dear Mr. Deane:

I know that you are wondering why I don't write and thank you for the five dollar gold piece which you sent me for my birthday.

I was so busy in school that I had forgotten all about writing until yesterday.

I will enclose an examination paper which we had last week, which I hope will help to make up for not writing. I am still anxious for you to come and see me march in the parade

I deposited the five dollars in the bank. I have now about one hundred and twenty five dollars in the bank.

Thanking you again for your present,

I am, Your namesake,
Walter Dean Ross.

In case that you would come — You could arrive about the Friday before the inauguration and stay till about the first of April, because Easter comes the twenty-third of March, and we have a week of holidays after Easter. Write tell me if you don't think that is a good plan.

In my last letter I told you that I was reading St. Ives. I have finished it and I am now reading Nicholas Nickleby.

Dear Mr. Deane:

I want to thank y[ou]
th[e] fine dictiona[ry]
you sent me fo[r]
It is just what I
wanted for a [long time]
I hope that you [and]
Mrs. Deane had a [Merry]
Christmas for we

are quite lonely now

I do hope that you and
Mrs. Warren will get time
to come to Washington very
soon.
Thanking you again
for the present that you
sent.
From your namesake
Warren

have not decided yet whether
to take up painting or long distance
running, I want to see what
I can do first.
There is a boy here in the
Post Office Department who is
from Massachusetts. He has
been telling me a number
of things about Worcester
Academy and Harvard.
His father is principal of
the High School of one of
the cities about forty miles
out of Boston.
He went back
Tuesday, so we

[March 6, 1914]

My dear Mrs. & Mr. Dane,

You seem so much nearer to us than ever before since Dane has left us that I feel I must try to take his place & write to you.

As you probably know face for the last time yesterday.

The beautiful golden roses which you sent remained with Dane & were the last thing we saw. Our memories are so dear of him & we cherish them so tenderly.

With the dearest love from the whole family &c.
from Martha

the end was instantaneous & we are happy that he did not know that he was going for he loved us all so much that he would have hated to go away from us all.

lost that our heartache for him in his solitude.

Papa & Mama are so brave & strong before us all but their poor hearts are bleeding

for as I were away we could not get home until

THE WESTERN COLLEGE
OXFORD, OHIO

attending is

there but it is
hard to understand just

97 Peabody Hall　Sunday,
Western College　April 18, 1914.
Oxford, Ohio

Dear Mr. Deane,

Your letter came to me while I was away on my vacation and since I have been back I have been studying so hard that I

will be either Smith or [illegible].

Yes I am nineteen and Joe is twenty-five years old. Joe is very much interested in stock raising this spring and is [illegible] of his farming.

We have [illegible] so in [illegible] [illegible] until [illegible]

From nine to ten o'clock

This is my last year of French 2, (my third year)

room. It certainly is quiet tonight but once in a while I can hear some one across the court laughing.

My piano teacher is the wife of Mr. Edgar Stillman Kelley who is quite a composer. At present he is ill

symphony," The

1812 Calvert St.,
Washington D.C.,
May 16, 1915.

My dear Mr. Deane,

Our letters must have crossed because I received yours the day I sent mine.

We are all well now, altho Mamma has not been well this last week

of war in his sermons, quite wisely so.

George is studying harder than usual for the last rap of the year is almost over.

We all send you our dearest love,

From Martha.

traveller will & return to us again—

We certainly enjoyed the prints and the [sunset?] back-sweet memories of your never-to-be-forgotten visit. Next year when you all come again we will do many other things and walk thro "Peacock

the service at three-thirty-Special Cars were chartered to bring the children from [mission church?] (& changed) over from [your town?]—There about a hundred and fifty children of the Washington Orphanage sang for us. It was a beautiful service — indeed each club

(ans'd March 9/14)   March 6. 1914

Dear Mr. Deane,

I am writing to you first of all. The beautiful golden roses which you sent were laid at the head of the casket when it was closed at the house and with those which his grandfather mother sent were buried with him.

Mr. Hannaford our assistant pastor gave a most beautiful prayer at the house. He said that it was from his heart. Dr. Wood our pastor read the service at the church and spoke beautifully of Walter Deane. The things which he said were not stereotyped.

was a little girl and always loved dearly, was visiting us. On Sunday night Walter Deane did not go to the church to vespers but stayed at home and we sat around the fire in the library and talked pleasant talked. Walter Deane went out to Belmont on Monday morning and called back good-byes there. We were sitting at the lunch table, Mr. Wendell bill - George and my mother — I when my mother was called to the telephone. We did not know certainly until we reached Georgetown that he had been killed. Dr. Fry who brought Walter Deane into the world was there also and took my mother back with him.

The ground is white with snow to-night. It has fallen all day.
My very dearest love for you and Mrs. Deane.
Rebecca Gross

he spoke of his purity, of his loyalty, of his sweetness. The things which he said were true. Mr. Breskamp, who had been the asst pastor for two years and who had been very intimately associated with Walter Deam gave the prayer. They said that his body shook like a leaf for a moment before he began. Mr. Hanna gave the benediction. The two companies of cadets were at the church. Their arms were stacked outside and the officers were waiting outside when we came. This was their request. He was carried by the seven boys who were left in his squad.

Martha and Joe went to the high school to-day. Mrs. Westcott the principal said every this woman who helped in the dining room at school were at the services. She said that never before had she seen them show such feeling.

We tried to make people feel that there was nothing wrong or cruel about this. I do not think that God could have been more merciful or kind. I can not help but feel that perhaps his life may help some other boys. A Mrs. Abernathy in the service of whose son Walter Deam died said that her boy had been changed from a careless wreckless boy into a man. My mother's cousin Howard Vander bilt with whom she had played when she

March 10, 1914.

Dear Mr. Deane,

Somehow I haven't the heart to write to anyone but you. I think if you had been here during the past week you would not have been sorry that you had given your name for my brother. At Sunday School Sunday morning they held a memorial for Walter Deane. Mr. Brackamph, the young minister who knew Walter Deane so well came from his own church about two miles away to give a little talk about him. One of these things he said was, "Just ask Mr. Collier or John (the sex- ton and his son) if Deane (one of theirs

and stood around the wall. The room was crowded.

Martha and Joe were came home Wednesday morning at two forty. Martha did not know until she got here, Joe telephoned from the station and we had a fire in the library. She was very very brave, as indeed we all tried to be, and she is is such a help and comfort. It makes me almost sick to think that she will have to go back but we will all have to be as courageous as possible.

So many beautiful flowers were sent and Walter Deane's body was so handsome. So my how all the [illegible] has been taken away although our hearts are heavy with longing for him Rebecca Rose

n't always willing to do anything that he ought to do.

My father sent Mr. Collus, the sexton a check for what he did at the church on Thursday, and he returned it saying that whatever he did was done as an act of love, and he wanted to remember Walter Deane as his friend.

Mr. Strong, Walter Deane's Sunday School teacher said that he was the most reliable boy he ever knew. As he told me this a month before he died, I think he really meant it.

We had a wonderful letter from Miss Wescott, the principal of the high-school. She had just learned how it happened. It seemed that Walter Deane stepped down to give his place to a girl, one of the neighbor girls, and the car started while the boys were on the step. It was a pay as you enter car and while the front of the car was not overcrowded the platform was packed with children waiting to pay their fare.

Walter Deane wore his cadet uniform and as I told you both coats were at the

George was baptized and joined the church the Sunday before [?]. The little boy next door who was an epileptic and whose mind was almost gone died yesterday. He was just [?] age.

March 31, 1914.

Dear Mr & Mrs Deane,

I thank you both for your very kind & sympathetic letters. I started a letter last week but didn't finish it. I am quite sure that you have all of the latest snapshots and pictures. He always thought of you first. We are so sorry that the latest photograph was taken when he was only twelve. I wish you could have seen him as he looked this year. He was an unusually fine looking boy, with a very fine carriage and a magnificent head. People have always spoken about his fine looks even when he was a younger boy.

Of course all this does not amount to anything. But one does love a beautiful body when you feel that the spirit within is just as beautiful. Walter Dean had beautiful eyes, bluish gray, large and soft like my mother's. He had a very heavy suit of hair. I've never said that he could lose as much as most men had and still have plenty. There is a little colored woman who is a chiropodist and she said that Walter Dean always greeted her as if she were a royal princess. Little Anna Jayne, four years old, whose father has command this spring of the battleship New Jersey has had a rag doll for the last two

She is about twelve miles from my grandfather Deane's. We are very, very fond of Martha. People say that she is a very fine looking girl but aside from that she is a girl of very high principles & ideals, full of fun and interested in so many things. Walter also worshipped her. He always came right home from school and he would always go up stairs to my mother's room and sit down there and read Martha's letters. She always writes us 2 or 3 times a week. George is a dear boy too and he seems to feel that Walter Deane's mantle has fallen on him.

Very affectionately,
Rebecca Rose

years which she called Deane. Walter Deane was crazy about little children and always had them in his arms or on his shoulder. And they loved him too. Lily [?] told me that Tuesday morning as well as she could for the tears that Anna had said that morning that she loved Deane and she knew that he loved her.

You asked about [?] Martha. She is with our grandmother on the farm in Indiana. She is improving it and trying to get it fixed up for of course during the last years of my grandfather's life she had not been able to do much.

Martha is a freshman at Western College Oxford O.

1812 Calvert St. N.W.
Washington D.C.
March 2, 1910.

Dear Mr. & Mrs. Deane,

Your lovely letters this morning gave us all so much pleasure. We are so glad that you are really coming to be with us next month. I know that it will mean a great deal to us to see you and to be able to talk to you. We shall surely try to make it a rapid visit for you and not a sad one.

I am so glad that Mrs. Deane is able to use her eyes - even a little.

This morning my mother has two such lovely letters, one from our assistant minister and one from one of Walter Deane's teachers.

I wish you could know how brave my father & mother have been this year. I am so glad that you are coming. I say that over and over.

I hope that you will like us all. You mustn't expect too much; I know that you would have loved Walter if I came and how he would have revered ~~you~~ and loved you too.

Joe and his wife Dorothy are very happy together and we hear such good news from them. We are so glad to have Martha home.

With dearest love for both,
Rebecca Rose

1812 Calvert St. N.W.
Washington D.C.
May 3. 1915.

Dear Mr. Deane.

Please take it for granted that I like to hear all the details of the things that you and Mrs. Deane are doing. You know that I am interested and we all enjoy your letters so much. Thank you ever so much for the notices and the place-card. Mr. Rand has beautiful taste, but I am afraid he will spoil you making so

[continued]

in it but it is much cooler than his heavy coat. We have been busy sewing this week, but we are going to wait until Papa goes to begin house-cleaning. This will seem very Southern and shiftless to you.

We all went down to church yesterday morning and the pew seemed very empty indeed. Papa's last Sunday! Well we will have to be very brave.

Please let us know how Mrs. Deane is. Tell her I shall write to her next, and of course this letter is for her too.

Very affectionately
Rebecca Rose

much of you? But of course we know he couldn't. Mother met Mrs. True on the car the other day and she said that you and Mrs. Deane were like a breath from the Other World. How is that for a compliment. Mrs. Deane's present came to day and Oh! they are so lovely! The colors are so rich and beautiful and I like the gold handles so much. Mother is so pleased with them and they will give us so much pleasure.

Papa is so proud of his handsome knife. You know that you both are entirely too good to us.

We miss you both very much and hope the time will not be long before you can make us another visit.

Martha is going on a picnic Wednesday with her Sunday School class. They will go down in Rock Creek Park.

George has gotten a black silk blouse to wear when driving. He looks ghastly

1812 Calvert St. N.W
Washington D. C.
May 28 19__

Dear Mr. Deane;

I have read the two articles that you sent me and I enjoyed them both so much. I think that Professor Bailey had the more interesting life of the two. I did like all that you said about him. What a great deal he had to contend with, and yet how much he made of himself. Thank you again for letting me see them.

We received Mrs. Deane's dear letter

The reason that I am making so many mistakes is that Mamma and Martha are talking so much that I get mixed up. I haven't been trained like Benjamin Franklin, you remember that he studied in a fair so that he would get used to working amid confusion.

George says that he will write as soon as his studying becomes easier. The competitive drill will be held next week and that will be hard on him but very nice in a great many ways. I will tell you more about it later. With dearest love for both

Rebecca Rose

to-day and it was such a pleasure to see it and know that she was better.

Mother and I played tennis on our 9th courts below the Calvert St. Bridge yesterday for the first time this season. It is so beautiful down there. I wish we had taken you down. But we will do that next time.

We thought that the snapshots which you sent were splendid. You must have a fine child lens. The picture of you at the cemetery was very good and I am so glad you sent it.

It is very cold to-night and I am afraid that we will have to have a fire in the library.

Martha and Ia are busy making sash curtains. We have a new kind of rod. It is kept in position by springs at each end so that you don't have to have brackets.

We haven't yet decided what to do this summer but my brother is so crazy to have us come out to Indiana, that we may decide to go

SMITHSONIAN INSTITUTION
UNITED STATES NATIONAL MUSEUM
WASHINGTON, D. C.

October 15, 1918.

Dear Mr. Deane;

    Since writing my letter of last week, I have learned that my father has asked Mr. Coville for an indefinite extension of leave of absence and two months have been granted him. Whether he will actually be delayed for this length of time or whether he is only asking for it as a precautionary measure it is impossible to determine until we hear from him. However I think it would be quite worth while to write him again at Guayaquil. They will sail from Guayaquil, at any rate.

    We had a lovely long letter from George, last week. He is very enthusiastic about all of his experiences and is working very hard on his Spanish. He knows nothing as yet about the new draft law. They are pretty well cut off from all authentic news.

    We are beginning to be very lonely and anxious to have them come home but we know that George will have to leave us as soon as he gets home so our impatience is tempered by apprehension.

    Mrs. Chase just told me that she is nursing a family of four who are sick with no one to care for them, two colonels and their wives. She gave her name as a nurse. We have been well and are glad to know that you have not been sick, either, at least with the prevailing malady. The city is quarantined to a large extent. But Boston is in even a worse plight.

        With much love,

            Rebecca

SMITHSONIAN INSTITUTION
UNITED STATES NATIONAL MUSEUM
WASHINGTON, D. C.

November 29, 1918.

Dear Mr. Deane:

    I have good news for you, at last. We have just received word that Papa and George left Panama last Sunday, the twenty-fourth, on the "Panama". They will be home in another week if all goes well. They have been in Panama for a week, waiting for a ship for all the boats had been taken off to bring the men home from Europe. We are so relieved. Papa has 3500 pounds of baggage. In their last letter from Ecuador they spoke of having received a letter from you together with twenty-five envelopes from us. This was after a silence of several weeks. Papa says that he has lost twenty pounds and at least two inches around the waist.

    Wouldn't you like to go to the Peace Conference at Versailles? What would you do with the Kaiser?

    We shall miss the kakhi uniforms here in Washington although it will be probably be many months before they are all gone. Have you noticed in the Casualty List the number of names of New England boys. This was especially true at first.

1812 Calvert St NW.
Washington D.C.   February 21, 1928

I sent card to make answer no [Rec'd Feb 23 ans'd]

Dear Mr. Deane;

We were so glad to receive your nice letter today. We have been so anxious as our doctors here said that Papa had an incurable trouble. Tonight Papa telephoned us that the doctors there were going to help him. We feel so happy

We don't know just what they have discovered or what they can do but it is so good to have a ray of hope. We will write you more when we have definite news.

I hope that you won't feel hardly toward me because I haven't written but it is the hardest thing I can do.

Very affectionately, Rebecca Rose

412 Cuyler Hall,
Princeton, N.J.
November 17, 1921.

Dear Mr. Deane:-

I have wanted to write to you for a long time, but I have now decided that I would even if it be a very short letter.

As you know I am a Senior here at Princeton, and trust that I shall graduate in June. If my plans work out I will go to Cambridge

Of course you know a great deal about Princeton. I have found it in many ways, as near an ideal place to pursue my studies, as it is possible to find. The fact that it is away from any city or town of any size is a great advantage, and one which I hold to be a much to be desired one. Of course there are many advantages attached to being in a place of varied interests such as Boston.

to the Law School. There I am counting on the pleasure of seeing you again. I have been looking forward all along to the prospect of going to Harvard Law when I graduated from Princeton; but until this year, it has seemed to be in the rather distant future. I will have a good deal to ask you about conditions in Cambridge, and about the Law School.

I have had a very enjoyable course here in Princeton, and have received a good deal here. However I shall be glad to get on to my legal studies, which I have looked forward to with interest.

We had the pleasure of meeting the sons of John Harvard here at Princeton two weeks ago. Father and Mother were here for the occasion, which they both enjoyed very much.

The Family has been very busy this fall with guests and other things.

I hope that I may hear from you soon.

With love,
George Rose.

I have been specializing in History and Politics, but such is the arrangement of the courses that I have done most all my real work these last two years of my course. This I think is unfortunate for I have failed to obtain as much from my first two years as I should have under a different arrangement.

I expect that you will be surprised to learn that I am not taking up my Father's profession. I have no leaning in the scientific line, in fact I have not very much interest there except a somewhat superficial one. Of course I am interested in Father's work, but mainly, only as such.

I suppose that this Thanksgiving will be an unusually important one in New England, as this is the tercentenary. Unhappily, I will not be with my family this year on the feast day, as we only have the one day. I will miss it, as it has always been an important celebration with us.

Tomorrow will be another big day in Cambridge. We are all wishing success to Harvard.

I hope that you are enjoying good health, and that you will continue to do so.

April 26, 1925.

Dear Mr. Sloane,

I was very sorry not to get some message off to you Wednesday, for altho I had planned it some days before it got blocked. I hope you had a bright and good day, and I wish you many others.

I am back at school after a week at home. We have the final wind off before exams which begin four weeks from tomorrow. It will be a hard strain I fear but I trust that all will come through successfully.

At home we had a very sad time. The day I arrived our good old Ida was taken sick, at the house with pneumonia, and died the day I came away. She was so devoted to us, and kind, and it was hard to have her go. She was practically a member of the family and so interested in all of us. She did not have much joy in her life so perhaps it is well she went Home before her prospective ills crowded upon her.

Martha is still in Florida. We are hoping she is making progress towards health. She tells us so much of the children who seem devoted to their aunt.

Joe calls the youngest "George Rosette" altho I do not know whether that is merely flattering the uncle or not. The two youngest children are dear children particularly.

We are having summer weather now. It is extremely uncomfortable.

I must close today but will write soon again.

    Sincerely
     George
   Yes I am &c R...

4826 Hazel Ave
Phila, Pa.
Dear Mr. Deane,

October 18, 1925
(Washington, D.C.
Oct. 19, 25) rec'd
Oct 19.

I am back at law school once more, altho the way I looked at things this summer I planned not to return. I had a hard time to make up my mind but now that I am here I am glad of it. I am finding my work much more interesting and am enjoying everything. there is a shadow in the thought that I do not know where I will get a job next year.

I was hoping to get up to Cambridge this fall, in fact I would have if I had had one week more of vacation but it ended sooner than I contemplated. My friends from Marblehead are coming down for the Harvard game and will stay over with me.

What has happened to Ivan? Has he gone to Chili. I want to meet him in New York before he sails but I have heard nothing from him.

I spent about six weeks in Florida. I found it very interesting but nothing attracts me there. It is so flat and uninteresting. I like cold weather and the northern scenery.

The things most interesting were my nephews, Joseph Jr. W.d.R III, and G R IV. and of course Dorothy.

Joseph is nine and a very wide a wake boy, thick set and strong but having a heavy body gets tired easily. He slept in the same room with me, and we two became very great friends.

W. D. R. is not as tall in comparison with Joseph, as he had such serious tonsil trouble, affecting his heart. He was bright and quick as the best. He has a sort of whimsical, mystic vein about him. Altho under size d and not as well built, he is the most lively of any, and has far more endurance than the others. He is moving every minute and says remarkably bright things

George is the largest for his size of any. He is the brightest and sunniest of all as to his disposition. He is so full of life and fun, and is a dear boy.

Dolly is a very sweet girl. She is very fond of school and of reading. She is very good natured. She is very bright and full of life.

At home we are quite well. Martha early in the summer had arthritis and Rebecca was under the weather but a month at the shore did much good for them.

Father and Mother seemed well after we returned from the shore. They are at present in the throes of having much of the house done over.

Do you ever see my friends the Watsons?

I am still hoping to get up north. Perhaps about ~~Feb f~~ February the first after my exams are over.

I will take the bar exams this spring.

How are you after getting ready once more for the winter's round of activities?

I was over at Princeton last week for a day. The place was most beautiful in its autumn colors.

Please let me hear from you soon

With love

George.

Sunday
(Philadelphia, Penn.)
Dec. 9/25

Dear Mr. Doane,

Just a few lines to tell you of ourselves. I was home over Thanksgiving and had of course, an enjoyable and delightful visit. It is so good to be able to go home. It is a source of strength to me, for I always come back, refreshed and reinvigorated, not through the rest and good food, but through the associations.

I found the family well. My grandmother who is spending the winter there has been having a bad time with her teeth, but all the rest are doing well. With our Ida, gone, they have found no one to take her place, so domestic duties are upon them entirely. They find it an advantage in many ways for the present time to continue as it is.

I am working hard here, and only regret that I am not able to spend all my time to my work, but of course know that I must not confine my self entirely but should get out and see people and things. Not only is it necessary physically in so far as my eyes are concerned, but also on account of need of relaxing mentally, and of interest in other things.

I am now planning to come up to Massachusetts about Washington's Birthday for a few days. This is very uncertain, but I believe that to be the best time. I want to come up to see my many friends and revisit old scenes.

Did I tell you my friends from Marblehead

came down for the Harvard game and then came down to Philadelphia, and stayed with me. I will stay with them if I came. I want you to meet my friend, Edward Upton, H. '25. He is a splendid chap. The game was not much to talk about as Harvard played very poorly. But I was glad that they pulled themselves together for the Yale game.

In less than two weeks now I will be going home, for Christmas. We have including the weekends sixteen days.

I expect that the Shakespeare Society is keeping you busy as usual.

Have you heard from Ivan? I want to send him a card for Christmas but as I have not heard from him I did not have his address.

Let us hear from you soon,
   With love,
      George.

4826 Hazel Avenue
Philadelphia
March 14, 1926.

Dear Mr. Deane:

It is nearly three weeks since I saw you. I have had a great deal of work to make up what I lost, and keep up to date. The last week and a half I have been feeling badly with a cold. I stayed in a couple of days. It is very hard to stay in. Otherwise I might have it cleared up before now.

I enjoyed more than I can say, having those three visits with you. I had been looking forward to seeing you again when I went north. All my plans for a visit to Marblehead included plans for having some time with you.

My visit north was very refreshing to me. It has given me a more cheerful feeling. I have not been as resistent to attacks of something resembling depression as to my work. My trip has cleared up most of that.

I was so sorry that you did not

get to meet my Marblehead friend. He is such a lovable boy. I am very fond of him. May you will next time. I am already looking forward to a return.

It was very kind for you to have me to lunch those two times. It was every bit a pleasure for me to be with you. Do not feel for an instant that I came to see you because I felt I should. I came to see you because I wanted to and because it meant much to me to see you, not alone for yourself but also because of the dear brother who bore your name.

I hope that you have not been subject to any of these colds which are so prevalent.

I will be going home two weeks from next Wednesday, and then I shall tell the family in my own words of the lovely hours with you.

I will write more later.

Please remember me to Miss Brown

With much love

George.

April 18, 1926.
4826 Hazel Avenue.
Philadelphia.

Dear Mr. Sloane,

I was very glad to receive your letter a little over a week ago. It was forwarded to me to Washington. I went home March 31, and did not return until the 10th. My sister's-in-law's father was ill so she had to go to Indiana. Mother went down to Florida to take care of the children. She left the day before I got home, and did not return until last Tuesday. So I missed seeing her which was a great disappointment. She felt she ought to go so we had to make the best of it. She enjoyed so much being with the children. It was her first trip to Florida.

Martha you remember went to Florida while I was North; but she stayed only a short time.

While I was home we saw in the paper that Mrs. Rodney True died the day after Easter. You remember we were talking about the Trues one day when I was in to see you. A little later I saw Mr. True, and he spoke of having received a letter from you, and seemed delighted.

The Spring really seems to be here at last, altho we are having some cold days. Last Sunday I was over in Jersey, and we went walking out in the woods. We found four spring flowers, dog-tooth violet, spring beauty, blood root, and wind anemone. The dog tooth violet is the only one I do not know as we do not have it at home. Of course plants were about a week in advance at home. The lovely cherry blossoms were just out.

When Spring comes I always regret living in the city, as I love to wander through the woods. Here it is rather difficult to get out unless you go for all day.

The family seemed quite well except for Martha. I hope that Spring and warm weather will bring her fuller health.

It is four weeks from tomorrow that exams begin. Then about two weeks and one half. Then all will be over for better or for worse.

The picture of Walter Kleane was taken in the summer of nineteen thirteen at Washington. I do not know what day as a friend of his took it and gave it to us later.

Next Friday will be your seventy-eighth birthday. I hope it will find you in the best of health. I trust it will be a well remembered day.

I ever enjoy hearing from you,
    With love
        George.

WESTERN UNION

CLASS OF SERVICE

This is a full-rate Telegram or Cablegram unless its character is indicated by a symbol in the check or in the address.

NEWCOMB CARLTON, PRESIDENT   J. C. WILLEVER, FIRST VICE-PRESIDENT

Form 1204

SYMBOLS
BLUE — Day Letter
NITE — Night Message
NL — Night Letter
LCO — Deferred
CLT — Cable Letter
WLT — Week End Letter

The filing time as shown in the date line on full-rate telegrams and day letters, and the time of receipt at destination as shown on all messages, is STANDARD TIME.

Received at

81D SY 13 4 EXTRA DUPE OF TEL TEL

WASHINGTON DC 1003A MAY 4 1928

WALTER DEANE

29 BREWSTER ST CAMBRIDGE

FATHER PASSED AWAY IN HIS SLEEP EARLY THIS MORNING

GEORGE ROSE

1040A

Hollywood, Florida,
September 20, 1926.

DEAR MOTHER:

I guess this is about Monday morning but whatever morning it is, it is early and I am going to write you as there is so much for those few of us who are not injured to do.

Yesterday between doing relief work, hanging clothes, rugs and matresses out, I had a full day. I intended leaving here Friday night for the north but couldn't quite make it. Also, on account of the warning we had I thought I should stay on account of the house. However, had I had good sense or known what I know now I would have been long gone. But I had no idea it would be so bad. It began blowing in the early evening and we went out to the beach to see the ocean. The city had hundreds of laborers filling sacks and building a sand barricade to protect the broad-walk and buildings. It was low tide and though the sea was running high and the wind was strong no one felt any alarm. But the wind kept getting higher and I again went out shortly after midnight and parked on the west side of the hotel. The water was coming through the arcade of the hotel so I turned around and came home.

I left the Dodge out in front of the house as I knew I couldn't open the garage doors. I then went ot to bed and tried to read the paper but the lights kept going on and off and I got disgusted and turned the light off so that if it came back on it wouldn't burn all night and bother me. Small chance!!

Somewhere along about five o'clock Saturday morning I heard Johnson calling me that the house was going to blow down. I told him to go on back to bed and stop dreaming but he finally got me awakened and I put the windows down in the front room and saw the Dodge down in front of the house. Ed had been sleeping in the back room and the garage next door and our garage had been blown away, also the roof on the back porch. When I got down stairs I looked out and the Dodge was gone! Later when it was lighter I saw it down the street and at various times it blew back and forth across the street but didn't upset!!

The wind at first was in the N.E. so we remained in the front part of the house. A short time after I had gotten up I heard the bang of glass upstairs and ran up. The roof of the house next door had gone off breaking all the windows in Dolly's room and the wind and water was coming in. So I shut her door and left that room to its fate. The wind was terrible, the houses shook and trembled and yet I felt the houses to the east of us were protecting us. The wind changed to the east and the tide was high and the water started to come in. We watched it cover the street, over the curb, sidewalk, yard and start to come up the steps. It covered the porch several inches and the house was surrounded with water several feet deep. Buildings were going down on all sides and no one could have lived out let in the wind, because of the blowing timbers and debris. We would see a dark object go flying by and it would be some one's roof, perch, or a cement block. Fortunately the wind changed to the S. E. and the tide reached the peak and started out or we would have been drowned like rats. But the wind from the S E was the most sever and I thought the house would surely go. The water was so high I fully expected the we would go floating down the street in the strong swift current.

About this time part of our reef on the south side went off and the water poured in though it did not make much difference as we had over two inches of water on the floors anyhow. Although it was then about eight o'clock it was almost pitch dark.

About ten thirty there was a lull and Ed and I went out the back way and surveyed things and it was awful! Houses all around were gone, the Methodist Church down and devestation as far as we could see. But the wind came up again and drove us in again for another couple of hours.

About noon we ventured up town to find the business section almost a complete wreck, postoffice down and buildings everywhere. Three of us went to the grocery and bought arm loads of canned beans, sardines, etc, and five gallons of water and brought them here to the house. Martial law was declared soon and everyting taken over. It kept on raining on and off all day and all Saturday night. They turned the hotels and school house into hsopitals and cars were commandeered to bring in the injured. I saw and helped with some terrible cases. We left the dead and only took care of the injured. My office was wrecked by water. I won't describe the sights I saw. I don't like to think of it.

Although I was wet all Saturday and Sunday I don't think I have caught cold and have been drinking a mixture of Jamaica rum, grape juice and lime to keep off the cold or malaria. All alch-ashol alcoholic liquors have been gathered in from the bootleggers and served to the people and it has unquestionably done untold good.

I feel that I have been very lucky. First, to escape with my life, second that I had $5,000.00 TORNADO INSURANCE!

The house must be rebuilt, walls and floors all spoiled. As we have no lights or water and sanitary conditions will be bad, the children mustn't come so I wired you yesterday as I did. As we will be far from normal here for some time and the lumber yards are almost a total wreck, I think that as soon as I can get my insurance adjusted, board up the house and so forth I will come up and go to the dentist!! I am afraid we may have an epidemic of some sort. Must get busy.

          Love,
            JOE.

1812 Calvert St. n.w.
Washington D.C.
January 6, 1929.

My dear Mr. Deane:

It was a great pleasure when on Christmas morning we found your book "Bambi" and the candy for us all under the Christmas tree. My brothers, my sister and myself went to thank you very kindly for your beautiful presents.

I had a most enjoyable Christmas, and I most sincerely hope you did. We all join in wishing you the most happiest of New Years. Very Sincerely yours,

Joseph D. Raff.

www.ingramcontent.com/pod-product-compliance
Lightning Source LLC
Chambersburg PA
CBHW051846300426
44117CB00006B/280